THE MASTERY OF THE BOW

By
Professor Emery Erdlee

dp
DISTINCTIVE PUBLISHING CORPORATION

Library of Congress Cataloging-in-Publication Data

Erdlee, Emery, 1911-1986.
    The mastery of the bow.

    1. Violin — Instruction and study — Bowing.
I. Title
MT260.E7 1988   787.1'07'12   87-32769
ISBN 0-942963-00-8

MASTERY OF THE BOW

BY PROFESSOR EMERY ERDLEE

Copyright 1988/All rights reserved/Second Printing

Copyright: The Emery Erdlee Music
Appreciation & Scholarship Foundation, Inc.
Produced by Ratzlaff & Associates
Cover Design by Danny Atchley

Published by Distinctive Publishing Corporation
P. O. Box 26941
Tamarac, Florida
Retail Price: $14.95

Printed in the United States of America

CONTENTS

DEDICATION

To my loving wife Helene and son Alan, without whose love and support this book would have never become a reality, and also to my wonderful students who I hope have benefited from our experiences together.

DEDICATION

ACKNOWLEDGEMENTS

Many thanks to Charles Pierson and Karen Ancona for their contribution in developing this book. Photographs by Lorraine Vallone.

FOREWORD

In writing this book about the "Mastery of the Bow" for the violin, I have endeavored to compile and collect as many sound, logical and informative facts about the bow as I possibly could finalize into a book. My mission was to help to clear up many cloudy, misunderstood and confusing issues on the various approaches to the study of the technique of the bowing arm. Also, I have tried very hard to avoid many of the pitfalls that some writers will fall into, such as the book being too technical, too complicated, quite confusing, etc.

With all this in mind, as you read this book, you will find that for every type of bowing discussed in the following chapters, I have endeavored to give you many different "schools" or "methods" for the solving of that particular type of bowing. They have all been carefully compiled from information furnished us from many of the world's greatest artists (both past and present).

For young teachers just starting out in their profession, it is most imperative that they realize as quickly as possible that every one of their students is an individual, with entirely different mental thinking capabilities, many different personalities, and especially, many, many different physical make-ups; such as short fingers, long fingers, big hands, small hands, etc.

Therefore, immediately establish in the student's mind that there is no rigid set of rules to follow as to how to hold the bow, how to use the bow, how to best produce the technique of the bow. However, based on the knowledge

that we are all different and there are some basic rules
in playing the violin that we should all become aware
of as we continue our studies, in each of the following
chapters I have presented many different approaches
to the solving of a bow problem, and it will be the
students' responsibility, with the help of the teacher,
to pick out the one approach that he, the student,
feels most comfortable with, and plays that particular
type of bowing with comparative ease.

The art of relaxation, flexibility, comfort and ease of
playing are the key words for complete success for the
future artist to be.

The student should always play as naturally as possible.
The question of what is right, who is right, which is right, is
where my different approaches to that particular problem
should be of considerable help to the young teacher as well
as the young student. "Right" is only good if it is natural for
that student and produces the best results.

With the writing of this book, based upon the various
approaches, systems, methods, or what have you, to a
particular type of bowing, the young student, with the help
of his teacher, should be able to solve his problems by
simply picking out the one approach he feels is the most
comfortable, relaxing and the easiest way to play.

It is my sincerest wish that this approach of mine will
clarify and help the student to avoid the many conflictions,
systems, questions and mental anguish encountered over
the years in studying the instrument.

Incidentally, many of the bow problems of the violin are
most certainly applicable, as well, to the viola. Possibly,
with some slight additional modifications, adjustments
should be made for the difference in size, weight, etc.

I must add my heartfelt thanks and gratitude to my
dear wife, Helene, for her encouragement, infinite patience

and complete understanding in putting up with me throughout the writing of this book; to my son, Alan, who was my biggest booster; and, also, my appreciation and gratitude to my colleagues and many enthusiastic friends in the musical world who insisted upon my writing this book.

Prof. Emery Erdlee

Chapter 1
MASTERY OF THE BOW

Its name derives from the fact that it was originally shaped much like the bow used in archery. The bow design in present day use was developed by Francois Tourte (1747-1833). It has a long tapering and slightly inward curving stick, made from the Pernambuco wood from South America, and a screw mechanism for the adjustment of the tension of the horsehair. Although it is now universally used in its present form, there was a 17th century German type of bow that had been recommended for playing Bach (particularly his pieces for unaccompanied violin, such as the "Chaconne"). On this type of bow, it was possible to control the tension of the hairs by pressure of the thumb, thus the numerous full chords in the "Chaconne" were more easily executed than with the modern bow.

The origin of the bow as we know it now is as much a mystery today as the fiddle with which it has become permanently associated. There was a slight mention of it in the Sanskrit, and from East Indian tradition, and we do know of its existence from many drawings and pictures dating back as far as the Eighth Century. Its development from that period, through the Middle Ages, through a succession of queer shapes, some long, short, arched, not arched, etc., to the present form which the bow began to assume from the end of the Sixteenth Century — all of this long period of transition, has remained a mystery. For example: At what period of time did the resined horsehair come into being? What fibrous substance was there before the resined hair? Was the sound of the fiddle any good? How was the idea of using hair from the horse to set the strings of the instrument into vibration ever evolved? How was this idea of horsehair passed on to succeeding generations of players in countries all over the world? These and many other puzzles are left to us by the dim past for future generations to attempt to solve.

It is interesting to note that the bow hair was so mounted that one-half ran in the opposite direction to the other half, so that the uneven surfaces benefited both on the up and down strokes equally. Long usage and failure to rosin often enough are some of the reasons why the hair will break frequently, so that in a short space of time it will need rehairing. Shortage of hair in the bow is a big factor in the warping of the stick and should be carefully observed and taken care of as soon as possible.

In the process of drawing the bow, the resined hair grips the string, lets it go for a fraction of a second by reason of the elasticity of the vibrating string, grips it again, and again lets it go, and so on through the stroke.

The rudimentary form of the bow was made of bamboo, which to this day can still be seen in India, the hair being awkwardly fastened at both ends, with permanent tension fixed. Gradual improvement came with the Arabs who gave their bow heads a point where the hair was fastened plus a notch at the frog. Along those lines it was probably carried into Spain in the Eighth Century, sometimes rounded, squared, etc., becoming quite small at the point. Earlier models must have been brought in from North Africa into Spain. Some crude bows are still to be found in Africa.

Prior to the hair, the Arabs had used strings on their bows, thereby producing a most "unusual" sound, certainly most unique, if measured by the most up-to-date beautiful tones produced by present day bows.

By the Seventeenth Century, the bow used by Corelli, Vivaldi and Tartini had almost advanced to its present state of development. A small screw at the frog to regulate degrees of tension was started at about that period of time. Tartini's bow being of longer length enabled him to produce the variety of bowings and shading of expression which he introduced into his music.

Not until the end of the 18th Century, with Francois Tourte, born in Paris, did the bow receive its last, and since then, unimproved shape. The Tourte bows are still considered the finest in existence. Some other fine bowmakers were Peccate, Dodd, Tubbs, Voiren, Sartori, Vuillaume, Lupot and many others too numerous to mention.

It has been generally conceded that with the conceiving of the modern type bow by Tourte, the greatest bowmaker of France, it was the opening of Pandora's box for Paganini, enabling him to open a new, exciting and wonderful world in the art of bowing. He developed a method of holding the bow, using freely every imaginable movement — in connection with it he was able to produce all the different shades of tone, expression and tremendous, dazzling technique.

The "average" weight of a bow is about two ounces, the heaviest part is about one-third of the length from the frog. The length is generally about 29 inches. The bow stick is round or octagonal in shape, bent to an inward curve, thinner at the point, thicker at the frog. The finer bows are made from the Pernambuco wood. The bow hair consists of about 125 bleached hairs taken from horse's manes and tails, although in the past few years there are increasingly greater amounts of bows being rehaired with nylon, synthetic fibers, etc., especially into the less expensive bows. These artificial hairs seem to last longer without being

rehaired again. Special resins or rosins, as you will, are
made for these synthetic hairs. They are being used more
and more in the orchestras in schools all over the country,
the cost of synthetics being less than natural hairs.

The selection of synthetic or natural horsehair in studying with a private teacher is strictly a matter of individual
preference.

A word of caution to young students just starting out:
"Never, never touch any natural hair on your bow, for the
natural oil in your fingers will cause the hair to turn black
at the very same spot where it was touched. No sound or
tone will be the result at the black spot." To remedy, use
plenty of rosin at that spot, daily.

It is interesting and most important that you know
something about bow pressure. It plays a very big part in
relating to your bowing arm. For instance, the working
tension of a very strong bow is about 12 lbs. The very same
tension on a weaker bow is about seven lbs. If pulled
straight, the very same strong bow has an equal pressure of
about 19 lbs., the weaker bow, 11 lbs.

Except for fancy designs or patterns at the frog, there
have been no real improvements in the shape of the bow
since the time of Tourte.

It is highly recommended, and I strongly urge and
advise, that to further help in the "Mastery of the Bow," the
greatest care should be taken in the selection and pur-
chase of a bow.

Poor balance, too heavy, too light, buckling in the center, unwieldy, uncomfortable feel, etc., are just some of the
reasons why bowing difficulties and much of the awkwardness experienced in playing can be traced directly to
the employment of a bow, unfit for use. "A fine bow, suited
to your hand, virtually plays by itself."

For the student, the aid of his teacher or some other

competent person in the selection of his bow is earnestly advised by the author. Remember, that if the bow is of Pernambuco wood, it will be quite expensive; Tourte or Peccate, running into many thousands of dollars.

Less expensive will be the bows made from other woods, such as rosewood and brazilwood. Recently, many experiments have resulted in a most promising bow, made from fiberglass. It behaves like a conventional wooden bow and is less susceptible to breakage, also very little warping. Has a most reasonable price.

The bow should be, above all, well balanced, elastic and its weight should suit the strength of the individual arm. Select your bow based on comfort, feel, weight, and no sagging in the middle.

Again, please remember that the bow must be neither too stiff nor too flexible, since tone production is unfavorably influenced by both extremes. It is a personal preference as to whether the bow should be stretched with a strong or weak tension. Your choice of bow should be between 52 and 62 grams. The heavier the bow, the lesser amount of exertion is needed at the point. A shorter bow is generally recommended for many young women players.

If the student is given a violin and bow as a gift, and if the bow turns out to be too big and heavy, it is suggested that the student hold the bow about a half inch higher up on the frog. It will be much more comfortable.

With the selection of a "proper bow," we now can turn our attention to the problems of the right arm, which generally causes most of the trouble for the violinist.

Chapter 2
TEACHING METHODS

The "Art of Bowing" was taken very seriously, and the most interesting and oldest known "Method of Bowing" was written by a gentleman named Francesco Geminiani, published in 1740 in London. The author writes, "The tone of the violin depends principally upon the right management of the bow. The bow is held at a small distance from the nut between the thumb and fingers, the hair being turned inward against the back or outside of the thumb, in which position it is to be held free and easy and not stiff. The motion is to proceed from the joints of the wrist and elbow in playing quick notes and very little or not at all from the joint of the shoulder, but in playing long notes where the bow is drawn from one end of it to the other, the joint of the shoulder is also a little employed. The bow must always be drawn parallel with the bridge, which cannot be done if it is held stiffly, and must be pressed upon the strings with the forefinger (1st) only and not with the whole weight of the hand. The best performers are least sparing with their bow and make use of the whole of it from the point of it under and even beyond their fingers. In the up bow the hand is bent a little downward from the joint of the wrist when the nut of the bow approaches the strings, and the wrist immediately straightened, or the hand rather a little bent back of upward, as soon as the bow is begun to be drawn down again. "One of the principal beauties of the violin is the swelling or increasing and softening the sound which is done by pressing the strings with the forefinger more or less.

"And lastly, particular care must be taken to draw the bow smoothly from one end to the other without any interruption or stopping in the middle. For on this principally, and the keeping it always parallel with the bridge and pressing it only with the forefinger upon the strings with discretion depends the fine tone of the instrument."

The author then goes on to write about scales, different positions, trills, arpeggios, and double stopping. For a first attempt of this kind, the book is undeniably a remarkable achievement; with some slight modifications, the bowing studies could be equally true and applicable to the present day.

Characteristic of the violin schools of the 17th and 18th Centuries: The elbow of the right arm had to be kept low. Campagnoli, in his method book written in 1791, recommended that the pupil bind his elbow with a cord attached to the button of his coat. This low position of the right elbow limited the sweep of the bowing arm, which, of course, explains the use of a comparatively short bow in the 17th and 18th Centuries.

Around the same period, the Italian style of holding the bow a palm's length from the nut, was used by many players, which naturally made the effective length of the bow even shorter.

One fine teacher's approach to teaching the violin was what he believed to be the shortest, most efficient sequence of systems that would produce the most significant results. In five sections, they are outlined as such: I. Harmonies; II. Vibrato; III. Shifting; IV. Scales and Bowing; and V. Intervals.

Approximately 16 years after Geminiani's work, Leopold Mozart (father of Wolfgang Amadeus, the great composer) published his "Violinshule" (School). Referring to the bow, he wrote: "To hold the bow with the forefinger and thumb more upright to the strings than with the hair turned towards the finger board, as by so doing more strength is obtained and the fault prevented which some player's have (no doubt, he meant the Italian players of that period) of playing with the bow so much turned to the side that when they press a little they play with the wood instead of the horsehair."

Mozart's Method Book was later followed by Locatelli, Lolli and Woldemar's; their Method Books' showing little or nothing but a great deal of what is technically bewildering to masters even now.

We now come to one of the most interesting and educational "Bowing Method" theories ever written and one that is certainly most applicable for all time, for all serious students, teachers and performers.

With a clearness and insight into the nature of the violin, the aesthetic fundamental principles of bowing were here laid down for the first time by that great Master, Tartini.

In the declining years of his life, in 1760, when he was 68 years old, the Master wrote a letter to one of his talented students, in which he explained about the bow: "Your first and foremost study," he writes, "must be devoted to the use of the bow. You must become absolute master over it in passage work as well as cantabile. The setting of the bow on the string must resemble more a breath on the string than a hitting of it. After a light start of the bow, the stroke follows immediately, and now you will be able to increase the tone as much as you like; after the light start there is no more risk of the tone becoming screeching or scratchy. Of this light start with the bow you must become master at all parts of it, at the middle as well as at the two extreme ends, and with both up and down stroke." He then recommends the practice of the "slow, sustained bowing, beginning pp and increasing the tone to ff, with the up and down stroke," and "to devote to it at least one hour per day, not uninterruptedly, but half an hour in the forenoon and half an hour in the afternoon," adding: "Remember that this is the most important and most difficult study. After you have succeeded with it, the lightest touch of the bow on the string will have become easy to you, and you will be able to do with your bow everything you like." Incidentally, the student, Maddalena Sirman, developed into a very fine violinist.

Sixty years after Tartini's death in 1770, two violin methods worthy of his name appeared on the scene, one by a Frenchman, Baillot, and the other by a German, Louis Spohr. Both books are well written by acknowledged masters of the art. A little later we come up with famous names like Rode, Gavinies, and, of course, the great 42 Etudes of R. Kreutzer, certainly fine bowing studies of all types. Many other brilliant players, like Alard, DeBeriot, David, Dont, Fiorello and Hubay, through their "Methods" and Etudes, helped to further the enlightenment of that noteworthy opponent, "the bow." And here we come to the last "method" of the past century, which could be described as staggering, super abundant, and yet satisfactory. Referring to that great Bohemian Master of the Violin, O. Sevcik, he supplemented all "Methods" by works as complete, each with respect to one special aspect, as it is possible to make it, all forming one continuous whole, systematically, progressively arranged, so that they cover the whole of technical development on the violin. Staggering in volume perhaps, but certainly a "Method" which would fit any student of average talent and sufficient perseverance and intelligence to reach the goal necessary for the performance of the most difficult Concertos, Symphonies, works, etc.

We must not forget to mention our present century of

"Method" writers, probably the greatest teacher of all times, Leopold Auer, who wrote a fine series of books for the left and right hand.

Along with this, a revolutionary, shorter step to complete technique and mastery of the bow — great books by Demetrius Dounis, certainly a most fascinating series to study (advanced player's only) hopefully cutting down on extra years of study and having to work on so many etudes, etc. It is definitely a most intriguing approach for the aspiring young artist.

Additional, more current "Methods" are ones written by Bloch, Kaufman, and two of our most talented teachers and brilliant writers, Harold Berkley and Ivan Galamian.

Chapter 3
CLASSIFICATION OF BOWINGS

Broadly speaking, violin playing, or the art of playing the violin, is divided into four distinct branches, namely: 1. Fingering; 2. Bowing; 3. Style; and 4. Expression. It is the second one which we will be deeply concerned about in the chapters coming up. As you will see, when the four fundamental bowings are mastered, it will be entirely unnecessary to study the hundreds of bowing variants which so often are assigned to students by their teachers. As Leopold Auer once aptly put it, "Pinpoint your problems."

1st Fundamental Bowing: Long sustained tone, evenly drawn, for 10 seconds.

2nd Fundamental Bowing: Frog stroke, finger, wrist action, no arm, side of hair.

3rd Fundamental Bowing: Whole bow martele.

4th Fundamental Bowing: Martele played in upper third of bow.

As we know it today, the general characteristics of all bowings are classified into three basic types: 1. Decisive; 2. Sustained; and 3. Resilient.

The decisive stroke is a sharply articulated or detached type. It consists of the grand martele, grand detache, short martele, dotted rhythms, staccatos, Viotti bowing, etc.

The sustained stroke consists of whole bow, partial length of bow, slurred legato, interrupted form of legato, etc.

The resilient type stroke consists of spiccato, flying staccato, ricochet, arpeggio and tremolo.

In the detached and sustained types, the playing level

coincides with the string level, while with the resilient type of bowing, the playing action is slightly raised above the string level, so as to permit the rebound, which so characterizes this type of bowing.

Usage of the bow for the many forms of bowing involved depends upon the need of the player, tradition, his comfort in performing these various strokes and the law of physics. Complete and thorough knowledge and effect or end result of these varied strokes are most essential. Matching the kinds of bowing with the proper division of the bow is the final goal.

The following is a grouping of the various parts of the bow, and the bowings best suited to them:

1. Full Bow: Long slurs, long sustained notes, long marcato.

2. Upper Half: Broad detache, martele, ricochet, tremolo.

3. Lower Half: Broad chords, accents, most heavy notes on, off string.

4. Middle: Detache string change, spiccato, flying staccato, etc.

5. Point: Tremolo, staccato, ricochet, martele.

6. Extreme Nut: Rapid detache on the G string, etc.

7. Greater Middle: All springing or thrown types of bowing.

8. Greater Nut: Short notes, short chords, slow detache on G string.

9. Up-Bow: Crescendos, pick up notes, begin softly, certain slurs.

10. Down-Bow: For diminuendo, heavy accents, chords, strong sound.

In the long bowings, we may consider these three different types: 1. The detache stroke; 2. The legato stroke; and 3.

The "spun" note (son file).

The detache stroke, a most important fundamental stroke (contrary to the legato stroke) is played by having various notes separated one from the other through change of bow, and by means of a pause.

The legato stroke is a succession of notes, uninterrupted by pauses, which have to be produced.

The "spun" note is a note sustained by a long single stroke of the bow, as much as two to 20 seconds long. The whole length of the bow should generally be used.

Chapter 4
HOLDING THE BOW
THE THREE SCHOOLS

Over the years, much has been said about the three "Major Schools of Bowing," (Schools refer to the different ways of holding the bow) the controversy being which of these methods is the correct one for you. As a young teacher, a doubt may enter your mind as to which of these schools to teach your new pupil — why not illustrate all of the various grips? The student will inevitably choose one, based upon comfort, ease of handling, etc.

Remember, a method is only a means to an artistic approach. It is not unusual to find the performance of a good player give no outward evidence of the school in which he was trained.

It is the writer's aim not to advocate one school/method over the other, but rather to indicate the real merits of each of these methods and what limitations attend each when exclusively adopted.

Let us briefly discuss the so called Schools of holding the bow:

A. German School

Putting the first joint of the first finger in contact with the wood and maintaining flat fingers and a flat wrist. As a consequence, the grip gives the player a very low wrist position at the point of the bow. *See photos 4.1 & 4.2. It is a familiar fact that most players of the "German School," possibly through tradition, assume a low arm position and pass from string to string by a hand movement from the wrist. Thumb opposite

Photo 4.1

Photo 4.2

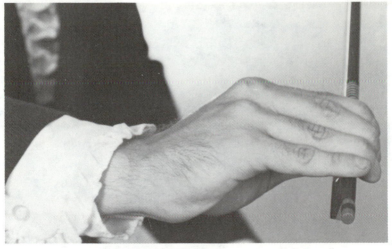

second finger, all the fingers are pressed closely together. *See photos 4.3 & 4.3a. The bow hair is moderately tensed. There is no pronation.

B. Russian School

Puts the stick at the top of the third joint of the first finger, nearly into the palm, with the

Photo 4.3

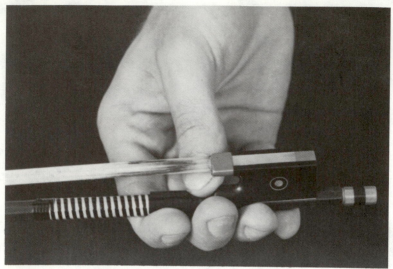

Photo 4.3A

hand naturally tilted toward the point of the bow, thereby putting the wrist into a rather higher arch, making it so much easier to utilize the full weight of the arm. *See photos 4.4, 4.5, and 4.6. The tone becomes so much bigger, and very aggressive, with more energy being used in the overall picture. Remember, the index finger assumes the guidance of the bow, the little finger only touches the stick at the lower half, the bow hair being slack. This is pronation. *See photo 4.7.

C. Franco-Belgian School

The index finger comes into contact with the stick at the extreme end of its second joint,

Photo 4.4

Photo 4.5

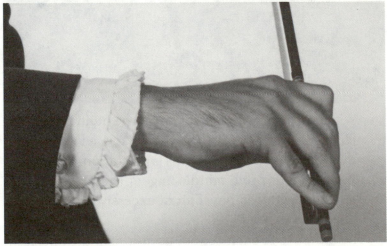

Photo 4.6

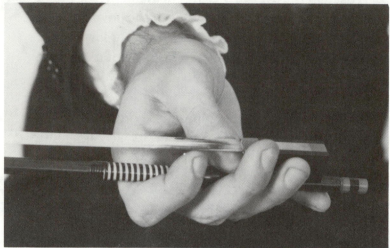

Photo 4.7

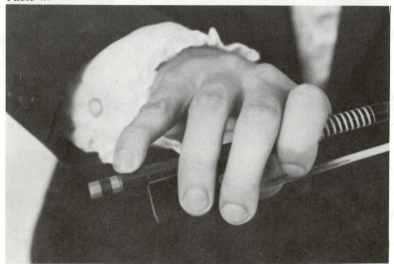

which is thrust further forward, the hand tilted slightly toward the tip and the wrist in a moderate arch. *See photo 4.8. This is pronation. Space between index and middle fingers, thumb opposite middle finger, bow hair at excessive tension. *See photos 4.9 & 4.10.

The old pure French school used a high arm position

Photo 4.8

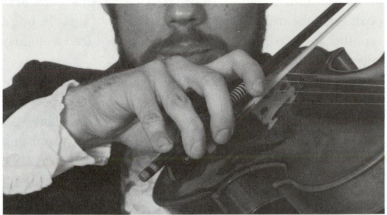

Photo 4.9

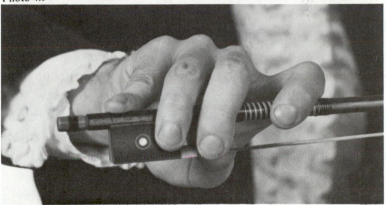

Photo 4.10

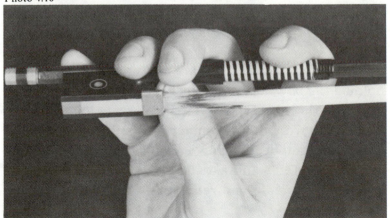

and less hand or wrist movement. With this high arm position, delicate tones were more easily obtainable, but a broader and stronger tone would have required a slightly lower arm position.

However, the players of the Franco-Belgian school seemed to have appreciated the merits of both schools and therefore chose the middle course, keeping the elbow on about the same level with the arm and wrist in passing from one string to another. By employing the arm together with the wrist, the arm is always in the plane of the string played upon. This arm position enables the player to obtain both the broad tone and the delicate one. Actually, the elbow is kept on the same level with the second knuckle, the highest one on your hand.

Sevcik and Leopold Auer were just two of many fine teachers who preferred the higher bow arm, rather than the old German School of low and clinging bow arm.

By now, I'm sure that the readers have come to the same conclusion, that the mastery of the bow requires much more detailed attention and development than that of the fingerboard.

Keep in mind that a discussion on these three different Schools of thought on holding the bow, and bow levels, can grow into an argument. When it does, please remember "that whatever means is used, it is justified if the sound is right."

As we can surmise, there are many added variations of holding the bow, all of them being based on or stemming out of the three basic holds or Schools on holding the bow. Once again, we highly recommend the student trying all of them and then deciding on the one with which they are most comfortable and satisfied. To play beautifully and with complete ease and relaxation, is that not what we all desire?

Chapter 5
HOLDING THE BOW

For more than 200 years, the subject of "holding the bow properly" has become one of the most heated, argumentative subject matters to be discussed among both teachers and players throughout the world, probably due to the fact that it is the most important part of a students' and players' study of the Violin.

Without a proper perspective for the understanding of what great importance the proper balancing of the bow plays in a student's tonal quality and also left hand technique, that student is not going to go too far in his/her studies.

In this chapter, we will be discussing the pros and cons of "holding the bow properly" — giving you, the reader, all sides of the picture — the "different Schools" of holding the bow — plus, the weakness of teaching the Violin in some schools. If you were to check the bowing grips of twelve of our leading artists throughout the world, you would be most apt to find a different bow grip from each one of them.

However, I believe that most of them would agree on this one most important fact: That the thumb and second finger should be more or less opposite each other, in order to maintain the best possible balance of the hand, the rest of the fingers resting on the stick where they feel the most comfortable. *See photos 4.3, 4.6, & 4.10.

A good teacher will agree that it is up to the individual to find the bow grip that feels the most comfortable, is easiest to manipulate, and is controllable with ease.

(The teacher should be ready to show the various schools/ methods of holding the bow, also, merits and demerits of each type of bow grip.)

As mentioned before, the precise manner of holding the bow is just as controversial today as it was many years ago, and as questionable as to how the left thumb is placed on the neck. However, the bow grip has been regarded as of greater importance.

The performer constantly looks for the flawless performance; if not, he seeks to place the blame either on the bow, too heavy or too light, or his bow grip needs to be changed. Naturally, as the years went by, the search for a "Nationalized" form of holding the bow continued, and gradually several schools of holding the bow evolved, such as the German, Franco-Belgian, and finally the Russian Schools.

The mere fact that these schools came about, with their different approaches to the bow grip, is ample enough proof to show the performers that there is more than one way to hold the bow.

Throughout this country over the past number of years, there have been many, many music teachers who insist on one way and only one way of holding the bow, even to the point of threatening the student of failing him in class if the bow is not held precisely like the teacher wanted it to be held. An experienced teacher would take a few extra hours of the term (perhaps after school) to determine which bow grip the student would be most proficient and happy with. Let the student decide; who knows, perhaps the future of a most a talented and gifted child is at stake here; the study of the Violin and the bow is extremely difficult, why discourage and hamper a young student right from the very beginning. This is the stage at which they need encouragement, in school and at home. An old adage says, "There is a hard way and there is an easy way to play the violin." Let us all do it the easy way!

To additionally nail down the theory that there simply cannot be just one way of holding the bow, just look around you at your fellow players, some of you are tall, some short, some fat, some thin; hands and fingers are long, short, stubby, so on and so on. Each person's bone and muscle structure is entirely different. Such being the case, it would be impossible for one individual to do precisely the same thing/way/method, as another. Therefore, each person must make the necessary changes as to how the bow should be held. The above mentioned Schools of holding the bow can, at the present time in our century, be most certainly improved upon by slight additional modifications of the hands and fingers.

Above all, remember, complete comfort, relaxation and comparative ease is the answer to your bow grip. No reputable teacher would insist that the student use his style, his grip of bow, or his mannerisms any more than everyone should wear white shoes and drive a white car.

A normal, naturally correct grip of the bow stick is of primary importance in the development of fine bowing technique. Putting it simply, the student should pick up a pencil or any other light stick and very carefully note the position of the thumb and second fingers. This is a normal position and can be regarded as the fundamental principle of holding the bow. The hand and fingers should maintain, at all times, the natural relaxed appearance.

We can very firmly state that the thumb and second fingers are the mainstays of the bow grip, forming the center of control, the direct line between bow and hand. The first finger is next in importance, being the pressure or volume control.

There should always be an appearance of ease in the

bowing hand, therefore, the bow should be held in such a way as to allow the freest play in the working and coordination of the finger and hand muscles involved.

Some performers like to play with a firm grip, others with a looser, more relaxed hand. Most play with the thumb bent rather than a straight thumb. Many will use more of a flat hair than an angle.

For a bow change at the frog, some will use only the fingers, some with both the wrist and fingers, and a few do not advocate using any wrist or finger action, using just the arm. The same thing can be said for bow change at the tip.

To test and develop the strength of the individual fingers, practice long tones, holding the bow between thumb and various finger combinations, while other fingers are suspended above the stick.

Thumb and 1st and 2nd fingers.

Thumb and 2nd and 3rd fingers.

Thumb and 3rd and 4th fingers.

Thumb and 1st and 3rd fingers.

Thumb and 1st and 4th fingers.

Thumb and 1st finger only.

Thumb and 2nd finger only.

Thumb and 3rd finger only.

Playing simple scales, this physical exercise will immediately demonstrate where weakness lies; for each finger combination should be able to sustain the bow in long steady tones — making sure that while the bow must feel firm and yet elastic and comfortable in the hand at all times, its grasp must never become too loose.

Another fine study for the bow is to simply place it on the open string, hold it there for two minutes, first in the middle, at the point, and finally at the frog — to be done on all strings. No movement of bow is required, just plenty of patience and relaxation.

To additionally aid in holding the bow well, try playing scales with the bow held one half inch above the strings. A silent but very effective bow study.

Four Levels

After deciding on a comfortable bow grip, the next step is to determine the four playing levels of the right arm. Without this being firmly established in the mind, the playing level and the string level would not coincide, thus producing problems such as muscular conflict, touching of other strings, etc.

Freedom of movement is an absolute must, and is possible only if the right arm is completely at ease. Place the bow on each string (at the tip), silently, with the arm remaining on each level long enough to convey to the mind a feel of that string level. *See photos 5.1, 5.2, 5.3, & 5.4. The bow should be removed after each playing level has been firmly verified. More effective bow levels can be assured if practiced slowly, bow on the string, then lift off, placed back on again, lift off, etc. Practice of this nature should be done at the middle of the bow as well as at the frog.

When tuning the violin, we sound two strings together, so that the right arm must now establish three levels. This time, the arm takes a position between the usual playing levels as mentioned in the previous paragraph. Once the playing position has been pictured in the mind, the next step would be the actual performance.

Many times quoted is the saying, "Bowing is the beginning and end of the art of violin playing."

For the very beginning students, simply holding a pencil (like a bow) before actually having to hold a bow, helps a great deal, because the pencil is quite familiar, while the bow is unfamiliar. The pencil is also short and light, with no balance problems. The length and weight of the bow

Photo 5.1

Photo 5.2

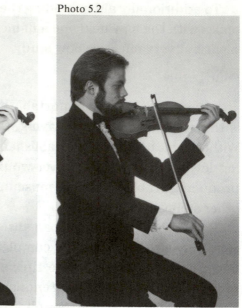

Photo 5.3

Photo 5.4

always presents problems to the young beginners.

To establish the shape of the hand holding the bow, some teachers recommend "gripping a ball" that fits comfortably in the hand.

Generally, the teachers seem to agree upon a four finger rule of index for the young student:

First — The bow grip is held with the thumb and second, or middle finger.

Second — He uses the first finger for pressure in tone development.

Third — The third finger is relaxed and lies idle on the stick.

Fourth — The fourth or little finger (pinky) is kept rather curved and rigid in order to balance the bow and attain a relaxed wrist.

The most common faults in holding the bow are:

1. The thumb is inserted too far through the bow. Photo 5.5

2. The entire hand is too far up the bow. Photo 5.6

3. The little finger is flat instead of curved.

4. The fingers are spread too far apart. Photo 5.7

5. The thumb bends in instead of out.

6. The thumb is positioned too far from the frog.

7. Tip of thumb rests in groove of frog.

8. Thumb is stiff so that the flat of thumb instead of tip contacts underside of frog and stick. This may stiffen hand action.

9. Bow is held by tips of fingers on top of stick, creating a flat position of fingers and wrist, rather than arched, inclined, vertical position of fingers.

Photo 5.5

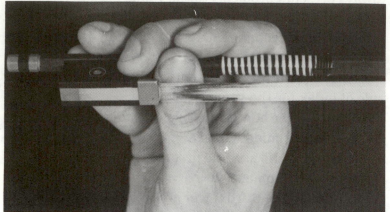

Photo 5.6

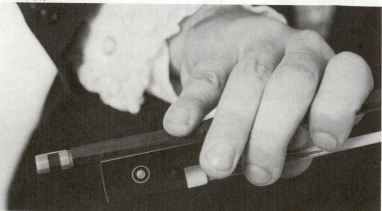

Photo 5.7

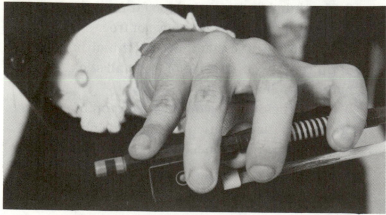

The Grip

Very important, but generally overlooked, is the material used on the bow grip. Generally, the young student has a grip which has been made from paper material, cheap wire, inexpensive fiber, simulated bone, etc.

Unfortunately, most of this material, in a short time, becomes frayed, unraveled, etc. It becomes a nuisance, a problem and most annoying to the young student. It detracts from his much needed attention and as a consequence, he loses his concentration. The bow must be kept in perfect shape from top to bottom.

Like a carpenter, your tools/equipment must be as good as possible and in tip-top condition at all times. The results will pay for themselves in the long run!

Some decent bow grips are the Thermal Grip, Rolland Boco Grip, and the Lifetime Red Bone Grip. Some artists use a real leather grip.

The purpose of the grip is to provide a slightly raised surface upon which to place the first and second fingers when holding the bow. Generally, there is a space for your thumb between the grip and the frog itself. The grip also helps to protect the wood from wear.

A most interesting bow grip for student bow control has recently come out into the field. It is a soft plastic rubber sleeve for correct placement of thumb and fingers, and it slides over the stick. It is called the Alshin Bowmaster, and is made in Sarasota, Florida.

Chapter 6
EARLY BOWING INSTRUCTIONS

For the young teacher just starting out in his profession, it is most important for him/her to first remember to find out the extent of the pupil's bow, especially down bow. Beginning students should never be allowed to use the whole bow, as it will only culminate in a series of "whistling" noises of all kinds, which becomes quite discouraging to the pupil, unless properly corrected by the teacher (also called "crooked" bowing).

Both of the great Italian teachers of their day, Tartini and Corelli, advocated the use of strings tied around the middle of the bow, the third of the bow, etc. This was of infinite help to the pupil, knowing where the middle was, where the upper third, was, etc.

Most important to remember is the parallels, so called "railroad tracks," the bow parallel with the bridge, the bow on the G string parallel with the floor, violin parallel with the floor.

The middle of the bow should be taught first and when that is well done, then and only then, do you move on to the upper half and the lower half, gradually working to the extreme ends, always making sure that the bow is being pulled and pushed parallel to the bridge. (Check Chapter 7, Straight Bowing.)

The use of the upper half of the bow will naturally involve the forearm; for the lower bow use, let the lower arm work together with the upper arm.

Teaching the use of the forefinger (1st) for pressure of the bow on the string can be next taught without much trouble, the theory being: Press the bow, pull and release pressure, all done in one stroke, result being, "not a scratch." Scratching comes from pressure straight down (without a release), however, it is far easier to eliminate a scratch later on than it is to get rid of a weak tone produced by surface playing. "The bow should always move with the pull." Use full bow for more tone. Notes with accents require use of more pressure from forefinger, plus more bow action.

Try not to change strings in the middle of the bow, it is unbalanced, lacks sufficient smoothness and quality. It is advisable to change strings, generally, past the middle of the bow.

The young student (at about six years of age) will have a great deal of difficulty pulling a straight bow on a stick which is obviously for the grown-ups. Small boy, small violin, small bow. Keep the little people playing only in the middle of the bow at least for the first six months. If the results are a straight bow, then, and only then, go on to more use of the bow — such as upper half, lower half and finally the whole bow.

Do not forget the much needed encouragement from the teacher and the parents that the young student craves at this early stage of learning to play the violin. Without it, they are apt to get discouraged and want to drop the study of the instrument.

"The French words tire (pulled) and pousse (pushed) are much more expressive than their English equivalents and the implied sensations can be felt when the small levers of the hand remain sufficiently adaptable. To convey this to a pupil is to ask him to take hold of the bow in the normal place, but only using the tip of the thumb and the first joint of the middle finger. He then holds the point of the bow with the left hand, and using the gripping muscles as little as possible, makes the motions of pulling (down bow) and pushing (up bow) with the right hand. If he offers a slight resistance with his left hand, an urgent need for play in the grip will be felt in his right hand. Repeat the experiment with all four fingers on the bow, but still without pinching between the thumb and middle finger, play is induced in all the finger joints."

This will teach the student the proper amount of pull and push of the bow, strictly by the feel of the small joints of the hand. Above all things, keep the thumb in flexible condition, avoid a vice-like grip and balance the bow instead of squeezing it.

A supple whole arm must never be visualized by the young pupil as one which continually hangs its weight on the bow and violin; instead, the arm plus the bow should be thought of as an aeroplane, which can be taken through the air without support from the ground (the string). The play of pronation and supination, tilting the point of bow up and down, can be likened to the use of the device which enables an aviator to make similar adjustments to the angle of his plane. "Landing" can be practiced with this picture in mind by playing long, separate down bows; the arm is first raised high above the string, descending some distance through the air before making contact very smoothly at the "heel" of the bow (frog).

Long separate up bows are best for practicing "taking off," with the arm carrying the heel of the bow to a place well above the strings after each stroke. It will be found that pressure can be best maintained throughout by means of pronation (although the arm is being raised), and the tone is thus lifted out of the violin.

When the palm is turned upwards, it is called supination. *See photo 6.1.

Turning the palm downwards is known as pronation.

Photo 6.1

Photo 6.2

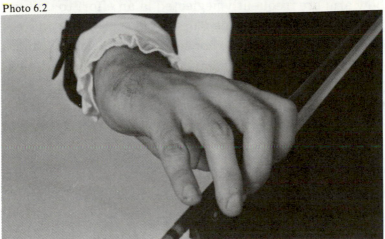

*See photo 6.2.

Pulling the bow from frog to point, the forearm will be turning inwardly, hand tilted toward the point of bow. The arm starts to turn as the middle of the bow is reached.

Perhaps the most serious fault in the average violinists' bowing is a failure to discover the appropriate height at which his upper arm should be swinging for the best tone quality of any given passage. You will find players using the arm at a height more suited to the E string when playing on the G, and vice versa. Remember the adaptability of the rotary movement of the forearm is mainly responsible. "Pronate the forearm — elbow outward, palm downward and to the left."

Remember, when playing, keep totally relaxed.

"We play in performance what we practice; how we practice is also how we play."

"Learn to totally concentrate on what you are practicing, always practice your pieces as if a master were listening."

The young teacher should constantly keep in mind that, unfortunately, the average student's right hand and bow arm are frequently neglected in an effort to develop left hand finger technique. The folly of such a procedure is obvious when we stop to consider that the bow produces the tones which the left hand prepares. Left hand technique is of little value unless the bow arm is capable of bringing it out tonally in an artistic manner.

"A part of the daily practice period should be devoted to bowing problems."

Chapter 7
STRAIGHT BOWING

Bowing technique is, if anything, more difficult and at the same time less understood, than finger technique. Imperfections in bowing are not so easily detected as imperfections in fingering.

Just touching briefly on another problem of the bow, to wit, "learning to bow straight," many teachers advise the use of a mirror. As a suggestion, place the middle of the bow on the E string, so that it is parallel with the bridge; draw the bow to the point by gradually dropping the forearm; then push back to the middle, also with the forearm, being careful all the while not to move the rest of the arm (from shoulder to elbow). Now, do it from middle of bow, down to the frog (nut), allowing the whole arm to move gradually forward from the shoulder and back again to the same place as originally, at the middle of the bow.

The wrist bends the hand gradually upward as the bow travels to the point, and the reverse toward the frog, being bent neither way at the middle. The hair of the bow will lie flat on the strings at the point and gradually become tilted over toward the frog, until from the middle to the frog only the side of the hair touches the strings. If required, a little pressure will easily bring more breadth of hair in contact.

"Draw bow always parallel to bridge."

Of the three divisions of the right arm (upper arm, forearm and hand), the first is apt to be overused by beginners and young students. The upper arm should not move in bowing except when the last third of the bow is being used. The forearm is used with the middle of the bow;

do not stiffen the elbow, for it will give the upper arm a faulty backward motion. The upper arm stays quiet, except in its third of the bow motion, and when changing strings. The hand is used to keep the bow at its proper angle with the strings and to lift it off whenever a rest or a pause occurs.

Many students often keep the bow constantly on the strings. The hand is also used in extensions at the end of bow strokes, so as to connect these strokes fluently. If all of the above is carefully studied and observed, there should not be much of a problem with straight bowing.

The straight bow stroke from frog to tip is the foundation of the entire bowing technique. If the bow is not drawn parallel to the bridge at all times, you are liable to have a couple of bad problems: (1) that it certainly impairs the quality of sound; and (2) the bow will travel all over the strings between the bridge and fingerboard, thereby again hurting the natural sound of the instrument.

Theory: As mentioned elsewhere in the book, your starting point for the study of straight bowing should be in the middle of the bow. Practice scales and etudes only in the middle of the bow, using no more than two inches of bow, parallel with the bridge. When this practice is fairly under control, go from the two inches of bow to four inches, and then to six inches, etc., keeping your eyes watching the bow to see that it is being pulled always parallel to the bridge.

This type of study, in a short space of time, should give you the confidence and assurance to draw a straight bow with ease and sound tone quality.

Chapter 8
TONE PRODUCTION
BEGINNING BOW TEACHING

Violin study is divided into three parts — tone, technique and interpretation. We will now start to examine the first.

Tone: (Produced solely by bow.) For beginning students, that is, those who have had no study whatsoever, tone work on the strings should come before the question of technique is even considered. Even with pupils who have already had some lessons, it is frequently necessary that tone be studied.

A violinist who cannot play a simple passage or even an open string tone, without some beauty of tone, is really not suited to technical study as of yet. In no other instrument is tone so necessary, audiences listen to the violin for tonal beauty first, and to technical efficiency last. For this reason, tone should be studied at the very first lesson!

The most important concept to be impressed upon beginning students is "that tone is the product of careful listening during practice." Do not bother about the position of the left hand and arm, but concentrate entirely on the bow arm, tone, in the simplest form possible, on the open string.

The bowings naturally divided themselves into two forms, the whole and the half bows, each being a true representative of slow and fast bowings. Begin in the middle of bow, pull as close to the point as possible (depending on length of pupil's arm), the stroke being even in pressure and speed, with the necessary pause during which the motion of the bow is reversed, being of the shortest possible duration.

At subsequent lessons, depending on how quickly the student acquires the half bow tonality (on open strings) the whole bow may be given very slowly, remembering that step 1 is the most important (middle to point). There are two reasons for this; the bowing requires only the use of the forearm, and strengthens the tone in the weakest portion of the bow. The important point is that the forearm shall be made to move freely with the arm in such a position that there is no strain, either up or down, on the elbow.

With the above under control, let us now move on to the whole bow. The first thought is to bring the upper arm into play in such harmony with the forearm that there is no appreciable change in the movement. The lack of this smooth transition of lower half to upper half of bow is called the "awkward part of the arm." To acquire this evenness in the whole bow will take considerable time since the pupil must be able to use it with ease even while thinking of other problems.

When the bow is on the string at the frog, it has the weight of the entire bow and the arm to back it up in its getting a full tone, but when at the point, both of these are lacking. Therefore, some substitute must be found for the natural pressure and this is, of course, an application of pressure, from the entire arm, through the medium of the hand and first finger. Remember that the desire to press may cause an unevenness of motion.

This pressure cannot be obtained by trying to regulate the exact amount by the feel of the bow; it must be done by the ear. Listen to the result of the pressure and regulate the amount by the perfect evenness of the tone. You will be more apt to train the hand and finger to the right pressure than figuring out the proper pressure before hearing the tone. The great mistake is made in imagining that this pressure is applied at one certain point in the stroke. Even at the nut, there must be a certain pressure and as the bow goes down, that pressure must increase, and vice versa. At no time, when the bow is on the string, is the weight of the bow itself enough to grip the string, and since there is always pressure, there can be no point at which pressure must be applied to counteract the loss of weight.

Even after the evenness of the tone is acquired, there is often a lack of firmness. The string itself is too often treated as something so delicate that to press it firmly would ruin it. Notice the bows of great artists, exerting pressure on the strings, by the closeness of the bow to the bridge. Remember, this is natural, well balanced firm pressure, not ordinary pressure, otherwise the tone would be raucous and whistling. A finer quality of tone can be found near the fingerboard, but the best carrying quality is to be found within a half inch of the bridge, sometimes even closer.

Playing at the point with an evenly distributed pressure and a pulling on the bow, not a direct downward force, will produce the best and most practicable quality and quantity of tone. But with all this force must come a relaxation that enables the arm to do its work with ease and freedom. It takes time to acquire anything pertaining to tone, and no effort should be made to hurry the gradual improvement, for it will result in the work having to be done over again.

A good tone is not a matter of so many hours of work, but is rather, the development of a conception of tone and the training of the muscles.

Listen, always listen!

For the young teacher just starting out, his earliest problem will be that of tone development on the part of his student. Most difficult of assignments! The first necessity is evenness of stroke, unless this is acquired, firmness and legato go for nothing. One of the most difficult things in violin playing is the moving of the right arm up and down in the same plane at an absolutely even speed. As lightly mentioned in a previous chapter, look at what is involved. First, there is the up and down motion, made even more difficult by being changed from string to string; second, there is a place in the stroke, when going up and down, where the use of the arm, above the elbow, becomes a factor in the motion; third, there is the gradual bending of the wrist; and finally, the keeping of the arm, as a whole, in the same plane, that is, preventing the elbow from dropping too low or sticking out. The first thing to do, however, is to get the simple foundation motion, which is merely moving the wrist back and forth, with the bow in the hand, on one string. The motion should only be about two or three inches, the arm held in its usual position and the motion done entirely by the wrist. The wrist should be so held that the hand can move up or down at will. This exercise is to be practiced in the middle, at the point and at the nut of the bow, as the strength of the pupils' wrist develops. The pupil will not at first be able to realize that he can move his hand without moving the arm; it is more a problem of the brain than of muscles.

It is of fundamental importance that the pupils musical consciousness be steadily encouraged from the very first. He must be made to sing, sing and again sing! The great Tartini once said: "To play well you must sing well."

The beginner should produce no tone on his violin which he has not already fixed with his voice, for only thus can he be fully conscious of the precise tone he wishes to produce.

The first lessons should consist chiefly of bowing exercises on the open strings, and musical notation.

The average young violinist, just beginning his career as a teacher, is apt to meet with many difficulties (especially bow problems) and no matter what his other qualifications may be, he is bound to possess one fault, inexperience. In the analysis of the problem, the young teacher cannot be expected to know how to meet every problem that may arise, for in his study, he has had the benefit of profiting only by his own faults and mistakes, unless he has had private lessons.

In any event, his experience has, at the best, been but passive, for he has not had to exercise his brain to discover faults; he has only been compelled to correct them.

The first and most necessary thing to be gained with a faulty pupil is complete ease of bowing.

Actually, in analyzing beautiful tone production, it comes down to three very important considerations: pressure of the bow, speed of the bow, and length of the string. Whatever bowing is used, or wherever bowing is used, the player must find the correct area to be touched by the hair for the best sound on that violin, that area likely being somewhere between the bridge and fingerboard. It is entirely up to you to find it. If the pressure is light, and the bow travels fast, the point of contact naturally will be closer to the fingerboard. The greater the pressure and slower the speed of the bow, then the bow moves closer to the bridge. Finally, the higher the position that you are playing in, 5th, 6th, or 7th position, the bow should always be very near the bridge.

Be careful not to grip the bow too firmly and at no time should you use the upper arm. Only the hand and forearm should be employed. This method, in time should give you a big tone.

A fine study for bow control and tone production is playing long notes starting very softly at the frog and increasing it to a forte by the time you reach the tip, then coming back to a piano with the up bow when the frog is finally reached. There are many variations on this type of practice, such as starting softly then to loud, back to soft, etc. Long bows of single and double stops seem to be recommended by most of the artists. It will greatly aid in developing confidence, eliminating nervousness and building up your nuance and phrase control.

Remember, finding the "right" sounding area between fingerboard and bridge is very, very important.

Whenever the bow is placed on the string and the arm is moved either up or down, whatever you are playing, always remember, sing, sing, make beautiful music. Even when practicing at home, play as if you are performing in a recital.

Agreed upon by most teachers throughout the world, the method of tone development briefly touched upon a few paragraphs ago seems to be to draw the bow very slowly from frog to point and back, making a crescendo and diminuendo in the course of each stroke.

Theory: At the peak of the crescendo, which occurs in the middle of the bow, the bow should be close to the bridge. At the beginning and end of the stroke, the bow should be toward the fingerboard. Strokes can be practiced on open strings, scales, etc., doing it very slowly, at least four seconds long.

For the very young student, the Japanese approach to tone and sound production is also very helpful. To wit: Have the student pluck (pizzicato) an open string, let it vibrate freely and have the student listen for the natural tone. Now, the student is to place the bow on the string and draw the bow producing the same tone quality as the vibrating plucked string — a natural sound.

For the most helpful suggestions for the very beginning student, make sure that the middle of the bow is mostly utilized, rather than the whole bow.

After the confidence has been built up from the constant use of the middle of the bow, we can now turn ourselves to the attention of the other parts of the bow. Probably one of the most common of all faults for the young student is "constantly running out of bow." In playing many notes in one long bow, he must be taught to "save" his bow, especially at the beginning, near the frog. He must be taught to "plan" ahead, realize how many notes are in one bow, then pull bow slowly, so as to fit all the notes to be played into one bow. The notes are to be played very evenly, making sure the full bow has been used.

In playing long notes, the students must begin either at the extreme point or at the frog, thereby giving themselves a "fair shake" at not running out of bow." The young player must be taught to learn how to divide the bow into four quarters, three quarters, two halves, etc. (slurred, of course.) Each note, quarter, half, sixteenth, etc., should receive its true value. For example, if the measure contains four quarter notes, should not the bow be divided into four quarters (slurred)? If played separately, then each quarter note is played with the same length of bow, no matter what tempo is mentioned. Always play with equal distribution of bow for the length of the note. To stay in the same part of the bow, the speed of the up bow would have to be three times as fast as that of the down bow.

The change in speed will produce an increase in sound, so you must be able to make an immediate adjustment to reduce pressure in order to equalize the increase in speed. To compensate for the sound in speed, moving the bow closer to the fingerboard will also help to maintain the balance.

All of it now hinges down to two main types of tone production, the first type relies mainly on pressure, which used together with a slow speed in the bow, bow near the

56 MASTERY OF THE BOW

bridge, will give you the best sounding point. The second type depends on speed to bring out the various shadings that are needed in the music, a lot more bow to be used without much pressure. Naturally, the second best sounding point will be further away from the bridge, nearer the middle, softer and "sweeter."

Chapter 9
TONE PRODUCTION
ADVANCED

It is universally conceded that playing on the violin is difficult. Why? Most people guess at the reasons, but few know what they are, even among players who have found it out in their own experience. Even the most modern player has a vague idea that the right way of holding and drawing the bow has some mysterious bearing on the tonal effect obtained.

The importance of the activity of the bow arm becomes obvious.

No question about it, the efficient management of the bow is indeed the most important part of the technical equipment of the violinist. It also happens to be the most difficult of all elements in the student's climb to mastery of the instrument. Violin tone is of a dual nature, resulting from physical conditions of hand and arm and of the training and psychic tendencies of the individual.

In violin playing, the individualization of muscles of the right arm is a perpetual problem. Upon these constant adjustments within the hand depends the efficiency of the whole apparatus.

Just to produce a singing tone, think of the complexity involved; every finger joint of the right hand is individually and distinctly active through the muscles that control them; wrist, forearm, upper arm and shoulder, through the sets of muscles controlling each, must contribute to the work of the hand at the right time and in proper ratio, otherwise the result is a failure as far as the obtaining of a perfect tone.

Not to discourage the reader, the problem is still more baffling when one considers how those activities of the bow arm must synchronize with those of the fingers of the left hand, which in turn requires an equally exacting control through an entirely different set of muscles.

Complex, perhaps, since the mind has enough to do in concerning itself with the difficulties involved in the music. It is quite evident that all of these muscular adjustments of bow control must result from automatic reaction correctly applied.

This is quite difficult to do, especially when the student has acquired many bad habits along the way, and this becomes emotionally mixed up with impulses by which one seeks to gain this freedom of bow control, such as affecting both right and wrong muscles at the same time and in most cases pitting them against each other.

Older persons will succeed best only through the conscious application of the laws of muscular relaxation. Children often do this unconsciously, which is the main reason why violin study progresses best when begun at an early age. For them, a certain amount of bow control ought to be secured before the left hand is allowed to be brought into play at all.

As once said, tone production belongs to two realms, those of technique and interpretation. The essentials needed here for the technical side would include complete mastery over the bow and fingerboard, skill in all facets of bowing, a very steady arm, good shifting and a good vibrato. All of these requirements, once accomplished, will finalize into the production of a fine tone. To go further, as the next step, what would be the general characteristics of all tones? The reader should bear in mind the sound of the human voice — a note that is sung in a rounded fashion will result in a nice round tone — a tone that is sung with a flattened position of the lips will undoubtedly illustrate a puny, nasal quality of tone. In violin playing, a similar nasal sound will emanate with the student pressing the bow on the string with a dominant downward grip of the bow. This results in the tone choking, creating very little breathing space for the tone. Even when a fragile, delicate tone is required, the student is more apt to draw the arm up and down with the bow merely following. Still, in either case, the tone is not drawn from the instrument and as a result the tone has no carrying quality.

The student should constantly keep in mind the mental picture of "drawing the tone." This mental picture will determine and help to control the action of the muscles of the bowing arm, and as a result, will inevitably be able to produce a round, clear and carrying quality of sound.

The student should practice short down bow strokes at the frog, lifting the bow each time, with an outward curve. This type of action will greatly aid the player in helping to garner that "drawing of tone" image. Doing it at the frog, then each time gradually increasing the bow length used, until the whole bow is being used, always, of course, raising the bow with an outward curve. Do the same with the up bow strokes.

Another fine bow study very highly recommended by many teachers is very simply to sustain drawing the bow, frog to tip, for at least 30 to 60 seconds, the same thing going from tip back to frog. First very softly, then loudly. This stroke will heavily contribute to the cause of bow control (during the strokes, breathe more frequently).

The most important part of good tone production is "listening to the effect of one's own playing, as though it were another's performance."

Theory: Though many modern stylists differ as to the exact position of the hand on the bow and the various movements of wrist, fore and upper arm muscles, etc., the broad fact emerges that to obtain a fine and singing tone from the instrument, the most essential things is that every movement of every portion of the arm should be absolutely free and relaxed, and the bow itself must in all circumstances be kept parallel with the bridge of the violin.

It is of vital importance to keep in mind that the name of the game for the player is that the bow is an implement designed to give to the player the "highest possible degree of sensitive control over the vibrations of the strings." The dynamic problems are subtle and quite complex owing to the many curious and variable factors involved.

The string is "excited" by the continuously applied frictional energy, which has to be of a certain order if an agreeable "legitimate" tone is to result. For example, in proper order of importance, there must be a specific range of bow pressure; of superficial velocity, meaning bow travel; good texture of bow hair, and in the rosin used, and a complete understanding of your bow's range of tension and weight distribution.

We, of course, take it for granted that the player uses nothing less than a fine quality of strings.

Theory: Some pressure is basic for tone production, but vary the use of the bow to include the making of a better richer tone by using wiser application of pressure, coupled with less up and down "sawing motion."

Tone on the violin is produced by a drawing movement of the bow across the strings. Its perfection depends on the manner in which a string is thereby made to vibrate. This vibratory perfection depends on the control, regularity and freedom of the drawing movement. This is applicable to every known bowing style, the vibrations must always continue.

The problem here is to renew the vibratory impulse, and

its effect upon the string, with such perfect regularity each time the bow touches the string, that the former sound of vibration is reestablished. The increase of tone is obtained by increasing either the speed of the drawing movement, or the pressure on the bow, or both.

As pressure on the bow is contrary to the drawing movement, acting somewhat like a break upon the primary impulse, it is more or less detrimental to the tonal result, hence increase of tone by an increase of bow speed is, generally speaking, preferable to one attained by pressure. This fact, again, applies to all known bowings, chords, double tones, etc.

Since speed and pressure are contrary motions which neutralize each other, be careful to see that the length of the stroke conforms to the intended volume of tone and to the required speed. "The faster the tempo, the shorter should be the stroke and the more moderate the pressure." In a fast tempo, the use of a great pressure compels the shortest of strokes.

As a general rule, a player should try to do everything with as little muscular effort as possible. In first attempts, this is best acquired by applying the law of muscular relaxation, in the form of a rest or pause following each muscular effort (martele) during which the bow is left on the string.

Theory: One must exercise wise judgment in the amount of bow to be used, for at times one requires but very little bow; an inch or two or less may be all that is required or available for a given purpose. The use of much bow in the wrong place will only spell clumsiness and stiffness. Thus, it will be seen, the subject of bow control is a very comprehensive one.

Please bear in mind that the natural bow weight is less at the tip and that it increases as one nears the frog.

Also bear in mind to observe very closely the shape of your bridge, how the strings are sitting on the bridge, and at what levels, for your bow to cross from string to string smoothly, one must follow the exact level of each string, so as not to "over motion" the right arm.

Tone production varies in character with each individual violinist, just as the handwriting of one person differs from that of another. There is no secret beyond a correct method, individual taste, and plenty of diligent, patient practice. Crushing the tone, by weight of the arm, should be seriously avoided, and guarded against.

Technique is the first requisite toward forming the artist, technique of the left hand, and technique of the right hand. However, herein lies the true test of musicianship, in a slow piece by Bach or in a perpetual motion by Paganini. You go to see a great artist perform his bag of "stunts." Several years later he is booked to perform in your city again — how many people would go again to see him perform his "stunts?"

The man with the mastery of his instrument, who is poetic, is the one who ever attracts. The man with the singing, sensuous tone of infinite coloring, with the delicate touch; the man who is imaginative, who sings and breathes, and cries on his instrument — that is the man who makes people think things they have never before dreamed of, this is the artist the world worships and will go again and again to hear!

Theory: A very important thought is to stop being slaves of tradition, both as to fingering and, especially, to bowing. If the fingering in your score does not help or suit your hand, for heavens sake, change it, try another set of finger patterns, and still other sets, until you come across a pattern you feel most comfortable with and play with ease!

The same thinking will apply to bowing. Many players

will start every measure with a down bow — why? Musically, this may not be good. Many times, one should start up bow, even at the beginning of a measure. Certainly, playing a down bow when starting forte and finishing at the point for an indicated piano would be in very good taste; however, it would also be more natural to make a crescendo with an up bow. Then why, after all of this, do we still continue playing, bowing, so that the crescendo is on the down bow? Tradition? Printer's error? (Does not apply in orchestra.)

I would most heartily recommend to my more advanced players and teachers to restudy the works that they have been playing for years, thereby, perhaps, opening their eyes and achieving a more musical result. Make the necessary changes in bowing if you have to, don't stick with so called "tradition." It will most certainly be worth your while!

No question that, in recent years, violinists have made great strides forward technically in the left hand, but the right arm has not kept pace. Why? In talking to teachers and students alike, I found that a very large emphasis is put on the left hand. Again, why? We all know that it requires much more knowhow and infinite patience to teach the various bowings and most importantly, bow production!

So, a beautiful tone, good technique, controlled relaxation, complete comfort in playing, that, dear readers, is "tradition." Not so?

Theory: Players have a tendency to play more forte in the lower than in the upper part of the bow, because of the fact that the bow is so much heavier at the nut. In any sort of crescendo, pressure must come from the hand alone, certainly not from the arm or shoulder, remembering that the greater the pressure, the greater the speed. As is well known, there are three fundamental factors involved for the right arm: (1) Pressure on strings; (2) Speed of bow; and (3) The point of contact between bow and string.

Important notes to remember: To play double stops requires much more pressure than on a single string, the exception being in the upper register, the bow pressure must be light, otherwise the tone becomes rather shrill and hard.

Slower speed, constant pressure, you must move towards the bridge.

Increase of speed, constant pressure, make move towards the fingerboard.

Less pressure, constant speed, move towards fingerboard.

More pressure, constant speed, move towards the bridge.

Theory: We will all agree that tone quality depends on a free uninterrupted vibration of the string, bow pressure not too strong for it may cause the vibrations to come to a halt. Also, bow pressure not too weak, or the vibration will also die away from lack of impetus. Compromise, experiment between the two pressures.

Theory: More pressure and less bow on the lower strings than on the higher strings is generally more desired. See to it that the index finger is maintained on the stick with surety, as if it was glued to it, for herewith lies the answer of more pressure, less pressure, etc. You must be made aware of the attachment of your index finger to the stick. Everything depends on it for the ultimate in tone production — quality, shading, nuance, technique, vibration of strings, expressiveness, dynamics, etc. Your goal should be to find just the right amount of pressure, not too much, not too little! Remember that the violin, above all other instruments, is capable of so many more varied tone colors, shadings, etc.

Theory: A very important adjunct to tone production is a careful study of the portato bowing, also called palante and parlando. They mean to speak, expressing yourself with a smooth pulsating sound, slightly accentuating each note, finger pressure only, no arm or hand. This type of bowing will certainly help to develop a large beautiful singing tone. Actually, the bowing is betwixt the legato and staccato, the bow moving along without interruption, no stopping. Also, practice with vibrato on each pulsated note. No question, this type of bowing has great expressive effect. Remember, three quarters of the bowing is done on the bridge side.

Theory: Relating to tone sounds that are unpleasant to listen to, probably the number one culprit would be scratching. When it occurs in the middle of the bow or in the upper half of the bow, it is probably caused by too much roughness, crudeness and insensitiveness to the pressure exerted by the forearm. Pay special attention to the elbow, possibly too low, or to the complete relaxation of the knuckle and second joint of the first finger. If the scratching occurs in the lower part of the bow, it is caused by too heavy a bow pressure! Check on the little finger, make very sure that it is fully resting on the stick, especially at the lower half of the bow. It is badly needed for the balancing of the bow.

Playing very close to the bridge, with too much pressure, may create a hard scratchy tone, but by the same token, if the bow is too far from the bridge, the tone can be dull with poor vibrancy. A very boring dull sound will also result from playing too near the fingerboard, especially when a vibrant sound may be required.

So, in the overall picture, we come to the conclusion that contact between the first finger and the bow stick is essential for an even tone production and clarity of technique. For the big strong tone; correct balance between bow speed and pressure, distance of the bow from the bridge and controlled muscular effort in the right arm, hand and fingers. We do know now that good tone production is very much dependent upon two things, the relaxed springlike action of the arm and bow, and the motion of the stroke at right angles to the length of the string.

Many teachers agree upon the three most important factors of tone production, to wit: pressure, speed and the sounding point.

Theory: Let us just speak briefly on the first one. Pressure: Following the rules of leverage, keep in mind the bow is heaviest at the frog, therefore, strongest at the lower half of bow. It is lightest at the point, undoubtedly weakest at the upper half. To produce an even tone, pressure should be stronger at the upper half to counteract the loss of weight at the point, and by the same token, decrease pressure toward the frog, where the bow is heaviest.

Greater speed of the bow will give you a sound of greater energy. For a tone that needs the same dynamic sound throughout, the bow should be pulled at equalized speed from frog to point. Logically speaking, a well controlled speed division of the bow is of the greatest importance in producing a fine tone.

Sounding point is the spot on the string where the placement of the bow will produce the best tonal results. Tie all of this in with pressure and speed, properly executed, and indeed, the result is a lovely tone.

A serious student, with good technical equipment, sound musical instinct, and a good ear, will achieve a certain degree of proficiency at which he will find the right sounding point instinctively by feeling the way toward and away from the bridge.

At all times in practicing or performing, make doubly sure your bowing arm is completely relaxed, especially at the shoulder. If the arm is tight, the tone will be "tight." It is the task of the right hand to set the strings themselves vibrating. Regular vibrations produce a nice even tone — irregular vibrations — you have noise, scratching, etc.

You must be very alert to the fact that when there is too much pressure from the index finger of the right hand, the string will be prevented from vibrating and you lose a lot of your natural sound.

Since the bow is much heavier at the lower half, it will become less index finger pressure and more counter pressure of the fourth finger. Now, because of the equal distribution of the weight in the right arm, you should have a healthy sound. (As you continue reading on, the various schools, theories in some instances, may seem to be quite similar in their approaches and in some instances quite dissimilar.) "Try them all, then decide for yourself."

Theory: It is most important to remember the pronation of the arm (outward turning of the elbow away from the body, top of hand tilted flatter to the floor). In supination of the arm, the elbow is closer to the body, the hand not so flat as before. Your down bows will be pronated and your up bows supinated.

As you start the down bow at the frog, your stick is tilted toward the fingerboard, as you reach the middle of the stick, the bow should start to tilt toward the bridge, and at the point, the bow should be virtually flat. (This helps to equalize the tone.) Going up bow, simply reverse the procedure — at the point, flat — at the middle, start to tilt — at the frog, the bow is tilted toward fingerboard.

Strict adherence to the daily pratice of the full bow marcato stroke will certainly guarantee you the production of a fine tone to its highest degree.

Chapter 10
STROKING OF THE BOW

Theory: There is a general misconception on the part of many young students as to the correct use of the bow arm. They are taught that the sign ⊓ is down bow and the sign V is up bow, that would be correct as far as the music is concerned, but the French put it correctly, "pousser and tirer," meaning to push and to draw or pull, or push and pull. To make it clearer, in playing long detache notes, for example, the stroke becomes a pulling and pushing stroke. It is of the utmost importance that the young people understand the theory behind this, for in the overall picture, if the stroking is done incorrectly, the tone becomes adversely affected.

    A. The full stroke is made with the entire length of the bow and engages the upper and lower arm and the hand. The great importance of this stroke becomes even more apparent when one has to employ the full bow marcato, or legato, and that staccato stroke of special vigor known as "la grand detache."

The player must have a definite idea beforehand as to which part of the bow he means to employ, length of bow, type of bowing, etc. All of this is based upon the time value of notes, type of notes or combination of notes used in the passage or piece.

Of considerable value in the interpretation of a composition when it comes to various strokes of bowings would be to think honestly and say to yourselves, "Was this stroke used and played in this fashion in the days of Mozart or

Bach?" This should be thought about by all players in order to arrive at a close-as-possible true interpretation of the type of bow strokes used in the days of the great Masters.

If approached in this manner, one is more than apt to feel the composer's true desire to have the various bow strokes conform to his thinking, and not necessarily to be followed by someone editing the particular composition, who has written in a guide line system of bow strokes for the uninformed.

B. The upper arm stroke combines the movement of the upper arm with that of the forearm (inward turning of the forearm). It is used mostly when the lower part of the bow is employed. No doubt, the forearm stroke would be preferable, rather than the upper arm stroke, if a choice was possible, because of its lesser difficulty of execution. The handling of the lower part of the bow is likely to show awkwardness and clumsiness. However, it is of the utmost importance to master the lower arm stroke. Special attention and practice for the overcoming of this seemingly uncomfortable stroke must be undertaken.

C. The forearm stroke (outward turning of elbow) combines the movement of the forearm with that of the hand. This stroke is used for the broad legato and firm staccato, executed at the upper part of the bow. No upper arm is used except some movement when crossing strings. The bow length of the forearm stroke will depend on the time value of the notes, dynamics, etc. Many players consider the forearm stroke as merely a lengthened hand stroke (because of similar movement of wrist in both strokes).

D. The shortest one bow to a note stroke is classed as a hand stroke, or wrist stroke, as it is sometimes called. The stroke is made entirely by the action of the hand, which is dropped from the wrist, for the downward stroke and raised for the upward stroke. In the hand stroke, it is very important that the wrist is quite loose and flexible, otherwise the forearm would be forced into the action, thereby nullifying the freedom of the hand movement. The changing of strings in the hand stroke is when an arm action is involved.

Theory: The independent use of the right hand is an important habit which should be established at an early period, for this is an important link in the chain that helps to make up the technique of the right arm. This is developed from the slight extension movement brought about by the enforced release of thumb in the bow, exercised such as the full arm stroke, grand martele, detache, remembering that the arm is more easily under control when the hand stroke is done at the frog. Holding the arm slightly higher will further enable the stroke to be carried further in either direction, regardless of string level.

The bow does not leave the string at the end of the stroke, but a slight pause must be insisted upon. No pressure, no undue muscular effort, no digging into the string, etc. Summing up, the hand release at the end of each long stroke, with the absolute must of a pause, will certainly help to greatly enhance the eventual goal of a beautiful bowing arm. Both methods of practicing the long bow, with hand release, off the string and on the string, should be done daily, quite faithfully.

Theory: It may also help the reader to realize that with a little bit of imagination, you can think of stroking your hand "over a fur coat," and then transferring that thought and feeling over to the "stroking of the bow". The general idea is to be completely relaxed.

That great Master, Tartini, had a wonderful suggestion for developing quickness of bowing, which I am sure many of the readers will enjoy doing, thereby reaping the benefits derived from this hand stroke. "Developing quickness of bowing depends on light contact with the strings. Practice daily one or other of Corelli's Sonatas Op. 5, the fugues, which consist of 16th notes. Practice them slowly at first, with a short stroke, detached, and with a little pause after each note. Play them first at the point of bow, after you have succeeded there, further down between point and middle, and finally at the middle. Practice them slowly at first, then always a little faster and faster, until you can play them with the utmost speed." (Sound very much like our martele.) You can practice above with any 16th note exercises contained in Kayser, Kruetzer, etc.

Theory: Another form of stroke that is considered a particularly valuable one is the Viotti stroke. This is practiced in a series of 8th notes, the first note played down bow at the point, martele, then followed by two short up bows, martele, somewhat like triplets. Use Kreutzer #5 as one example. It is highly important to practice first at the tip of bow, then at the frog. When practicing at the frog, lift bow from the string after each note.

Theory: The long separate decisive strokes have been acknowledged to have special value in developing control of the bow. The use of the whole bow, requiring the free sweep of the arm and involving highly vitalized muscular action, makes absolutely necessary a corresponding release of muscular contractions.

To enforce this release of muscular effort, many modern teachers recommend starting with a decisive up bow stroke, with the complete release of the thumb from its normal position in the grip of the bow at the conclusion of each stroke. This exercise is remarkably effective. The release of thumb after the up bow stroke permits the bow to fall lightly into the half closed hand.

The removal of bow from string is important of itself, aside from the enforced relaxation secured by the release of the thumb. To be able to break and to resume contact with the string within a given time and at any part of the bow, without hesitation of rhythmical values, elevates the player from the hesitating cautious class into the rank of the positive and technically fearless.

The drastic removal of bow from string will rapidly develop agility and strength in hand and arm, even with the almost beginner. So, the first down strokes should also be followed by complete removal of the bow from the string and a silent return to a position from which to commence another decisive down stroke.

Make sure you spend some amount of time practicing in the lower half of the bow. You will find the results of bow control most rewarding.

Chapter 11
BOW CHANGING

One of the more difficult problems encountered is the bow change, especially at the frog. It is most important that the bow change should be as smooth and as unnoticeable as possible. The problem here is that there are too many theories as to how this can be carried out with the least amount of effort.

Examples: Using fingers only — Use of the hand and wrist — Forearm only, etc.

Actually, the real answer to all of this lies not in the above examples, but in the ability of the player to keep in mind two important factors: (1) the bow should slow down shortly before the change, like a tiny hesitation; (2) pressure has to be lightened (only a 4th finger pressure).

Whether done by fingers, hand or arm, etc., is entirely immaterial; if the student's bow change is smooth, leave well enough alone, regardless of how he does it. With some students, it all comes very naturally.

If the bow change has jerky motions, then we must apply remedies such as those mentioned in the beginning of this chapter. First "slow the bow down," then decide, by trying out the various positions of the arm, wrist, or fingers.

Important to remember: At the frog, the 4th finger has the pressure point. As the bow nears the frog, imagine that you are going to lift the bow off the string, no arm pressure, only the 4th finger presses down firmly. At the point, reverse the process, first or index finger is the pressure point, 4th finger is off the stick or very lightly on the stick.

A good change of bow is inaudible and virtually invisible.

Sometimes lifting the elbow a little higher will aid in making a smooth bow change. Waiting until the last moment, at the frog, may also help to make a smooth bow change. Do not anticipate the change at the frog too soon.

Changing the bow at the frog in a double piano, use the fingers, with very little hair. In double forte, the entire hand performs the bow change with flexible fingers, using about 3/4 of the bow width. It is not always necessary for the little finger to be on the stick. (I like it on at the frog for proper balancing of the bow.) It is clearly a matter of personal preference.

Changing bow at the point can be done by the use of the fingers only or by wrist and arm combined. The most important thing to be remembered is a very relaxed, well coordinated bow arm. String changes should be made with the wrist and elbow at the same level.

Like everything else, there are exceptions to the rule; as one eminent violinist advocated, "I object to the wrist being used as a bow change at the nut of the bow, it feels like a little 'gulp.' There is an excellent type of control one gets when using a lot more arm, even in fast passages, I use very little wrist. It is important that as much power should be developed in the upper as well as in the lower part of the bow. The shoulder should play an important part. It is possible to play well, using the wrist much of the time, but it is better to play from the shoulder, with very little motion of the wrist."

Again, we run into different approaches and theories for smooth bow changes. Since, in the final analysis, our goal is to achieve a flexible bow change, one that is not discernible to the ear when it occurs either at the frog or at the point of the bow, it is up to the player to choose the fingers, wrist, arm or any combination of these methods, as long as the end result is a "smooth bow change."

There are a few violinists who rarely play near the frog area, or who do not push the bow anywhere near the frog. This, again, is an individual choice. Holding the bow further up the stick is another example. All of this, of course, shortens your bow stroke.

Chapter 12
BOW PROBLEMS
TREMBLING — NERVOUSNESS

The question has often been asked, "What is the best exercise for what seems to be a stiff bow arm?" In playing long drawn out tones, I seem to find it very hard to keep the tone even and the bow steady as the latter is very much inclined to quiver.

Tremor in the bow is either chronic or occasional. Since chronic is strictly a health problem, we will speak only of the occasional, particularly where the bow hand of the violinist trembles during the first few bars of the composition he is playing in public. But he will soon recover his confidence as his hand becomes steady.

As to the general causes of the trembling, they can be quite numerous. A few are carrying heavy weights, heavy smoking and drinking excessively, use of drugs, outdoor sports when one first begins them, especially the so called "weekend athlete." These and many others, too numerous to mention, will result in a tremulous condition of the muscles involved.

To help answer the question of the stiff and nervous bow arm, the following exercises have been suggested. (1) Always keep right arm completely relaxed. Relax from the shoulder to the fingertips. (2) Practice long bows on open strings, from frog to tip and back — first for 8 counts, then 12, 16, 24 and 30. At the slightest sign of weariness, stop playing and let the arm fall limp at the side, resting arm until all tension is gone. Then resume open string long bows. You should let the arm fall loosely at the side, as many times as needed when the tension occurs. Keep your mind concentrated on the complete relaxation of the right arm. (3) Practice these long tones as soft as a whisper. This should automatically cause a certain amount of relaxation. Breathe often during the strokes.

The story of how Viotti, the great violinist and composer, came back after having given up violin playing for a long period has become a classic in the history of violin playing. Viotti, after a distinguished career as a virtuoso, decided to give up the violin. He engaged in business as a wine merchant in London and did no public playing for a number of years. Returning to Paris on one occasion, his legion of admirers prevailed upon him to appear once more on the concert stage. In vain he pleaded that he was utterly unprepared to play at the concert which was only a few days distant. His friends would not take "no" for an answer. He finally consented.

The means he took of coming back was through hours of practice every day on long drawn out tones with long bow, with additional attention to much practice on scales and arpeggi, to get his left hand fingers in good working condition. Needless to say, so successful was this method of practice, he rapidly regained his former technique, and his playing at the concert was a brilliant success.

Success comes most readily when one is in no hurry to see results; nerves and muscles are unmanageable, exasperating and stubborn servants when you try to hurry them. By gentle persuasion and careful application of the laws of muscular relaxation, wonders have been accomplished, even with those of advancing years.

Many a stiff arm has been cured in that way, provided the sufferer is in no hurry to get results.

Remember that stiffness is not an actual physical disability of any part of the arm to move in a desired way, but simply a matter of a disinclination of certain muscles to act independently of other muscles. If it is allowed to go on, then indeed an incurable disability sets in and each succeeding year of playing becomes that much more difficult to correct.

Bowing is the beginning and end of the art of violin playing. Spend much more time practicing on the right hand than the left. Many students who have supposed their trouble to be a bad ear really fail on account of initial bad bowing, and sheer neglect of it. A faulty left hand can be set right, a radically faulty bow arm, seldom.

Exercise the bow arm daily in all kinds of bowings and different tone shades, then and only then, practice your left hand. Too often, pupils omit the bow exercises altogether.

As it is chiefly the difficulties of the bow which require special practice in pieces, the player with the right arm well trained and well drilled by daily gymnastics finds his problems greatly reduced, finding his mind fresh and eager to cope with whatever other difficulties the piece may present.

And so, regularity of practice, inseparable from regularity of lessons, is as much a key to success as talent. Without it, talent will not accomplish much.

Many of the great artists have their own answers as to nervousness in playing before the public. For starters, here are some of their thoughts:

Play long notes very, very softly, at least 30 seconds in length, including double tones, played the same way.

Learn to divide the bow into four equal parts; then mix up the parts, such as playing the first part fast, the second and third parts very slow, and then the fourth part fast (make up your own mixes).

To learn how to breathe properly on long notes, take a half breath, and on short rests, take long breaths, remembering that nervousness is caused by insufficient breathing.

Draw the bow not on the string, but above the string for at least 30 seconds. The idea is to play long bows, keeping the bow at the same distance above the string.

Practice setting the bow down on the string, at any part of the bow, without making any sound.

Many fine teachers seem to agree that the player who suffers from a feeling of insecurity when performing in public should be aware of the actions of his right arm and not be blaming his left hand. Unrecognized bowing imperfections are more than responsible four out of five times for scrambled and blurred passages.

A fine balanced right arm is well able to equalize unequal left hand finger work in an amazing way. "They assure all nervous, trembling players that control is chiefly centered in the right arm!"

Another good recommendation — when having to play a long note during your performance, you find your right arm starting to tremble, quickly tilt your stick toward the fingerboard as much as possible — it will be of considerable help.

Another good tip: If the bow trembles, try to push and pull the bow in a fashion of a figure 8, and finally, if the bow trembles, concentrate your eyes on what the left hand is doing — watch the fingers of the left hand!

Many artists feel that the daily practice of the full bow marcato is the best answer for the questions pertaining to trembling, nervousness, etc.

Trembling, nervousness, and tension still remain as roadblocks to a better bowing arm. Certainly, tension remains near the top of the list as virtually an incurable disease. It very rarely effects the very young or young students, but as they start to grow up, watch out, the looseness and relaxed way of playing is starting to be lost and then tension starts to set in. Problems start to increase and the teenage student desperately needs help, very quickly.

It is not always easy to diagnose tension, sometimes the teacher mistakes it for a certain high level of intensity and desire on the part of the student to achieve a more accurate degree of playing.

Major attempts or methods of trying to help solve tension would certainly contain some of the following suggestions:

(1) While playing, breathe more frequently, short quick breaths.

(2) Relax your stomach, arms and then your knees. We do know that technique and lovely sound do not require a lot of physical tension. Try to keep your entire body completely relaxed at all times.

(3) At every lesson, the student should be reminded of tension, the necessity of complete relaxation of every part of the body — arms, stomach, knees, legs, etc.

(4) The relaxing of both shoulders forces you into the complete loss of tension in the muscles of the face, neck, etc. Suggestions for the teacher would be to write "RELAX" on every single page of the student's lessons. You will reap the benefits from this sort of persistency.

(5) Arpeggios, crossing strings, different levels also have a tendency to create tension. Using the smallest muscle or part of the hand to cross should help to loosen the muscles of the shoulder.

(6) Using a shoulder pad will also help to

decrease tension.

(7) The loss of bow technique can most of the time be traced to very stiff bow fingers (sometimes labeled as "locked" bow fingers). The wrist, elbow and arm cannot be truly flexible if the fingers are "locked."

Complete relaxation at all times while playing is your medication for the solving of that almost incurable disease — TENSION.

Chapter 13
DETACHE
BROAD — BOW CHANGE — SHORT

We now come to the bow stroke that is called the foundation or the basic of all bowings; the detache or sustained tone, purely on the string.

Playing detache in a fast tempo requires less than two inches of bow, naturally, using only the wrist at any part of the bow. Holding the bow properly, in the sense that you must feel the starting impulse between your thumb and second finger, this eraser type of stroke would be used as mentioned before, only in rapid passages. In a slower tempo, same length of bow being utilized, the forearm and the wrist would then be used.

The large detache should be thought of as a brush stroke, somewhat like that of a person painting a wall with a brush stroke. The playing of detache strokes should be solely thought of as strictly a pulling stroke, not a pushing stroke. For example, the playing of a down bow should be a pull instead of a push.

When we learn this short detache eraser stroke well, we will now be able to study the fast spiccato or sautille without too many problems. All of these bowings should be done normally at the middle of the bow, depending, of course, on the level of dynamics.

Louder detache tones are to be played with the bow nearer the bridge using slightly more pressure and moving at a slower rate of speed. Softer tones generally, played closer to the fingerboard.

For the change from detache to spiccato, if the bow does not seem to bounce, simply lower bow arm and elbow just enough for the bow to start bouncing. Do not force the bow to bounce, never force, simply relax the entire arm.

To cultivate the detache to a fine degree, in practicing this stroke always try to attack each stroke from the wrist, using the whole length of the bow, in a moderate tempo, up and down stroke, attempting to get an equal tone. You may vary this by using the different parts of the bow, starting at the nut, then the middle and at the point.

It is the simplest form of bowing because each note is played with a separate stroke. The bow is always on the string and there is never a pause between strokes. Always practice with the thought of trying to obtain a relaxed natural tone, which involves a completely light inward turn of the arm, hand tilted to the left, elbow extended outward with a flexible wrist.

Accent the up stroke detache so as to even up the natural tendency to play the down bows so much stronger. Generally, a heavier sound occurs at the lowest part of the bow, which starts at the down bow. Changes of bow strokes must be as imperceptible as possible. The full bow detache is usually called "Grand Detache."

Practice detache at the frog, wrist only, using little bow. Make sure little finger is on the stick, with a slight pressure, for a precise balance. It has been suggested the detache be practiced at the frog, without the two middle fingers, only with thumb, index and little finger. Undoubtedly, this will help to develop strength in the little finger, resulting in a better control of the bow.

Detache is a word meaning separate or detached consecutive strokes up and down, played as smoothly as possible without any accents. The detache is the basic of basic strokes. Most of the other bowings are considered an outgrowth of the detache. When playing the long or broad detache, please remember these few points:

A. Watch inward turning of forearm, elbow outward.

B. No pressure on arm, just natural.

C. Relax fingers on bow.

D. The changing of the bow at frog and point has to be done very smoothly; with no obvious bow change heard.

In the fast or short detache, this becomes a hand movement, very loose wrist. Pay strict attention to the weight of the first finger on the bow. The fast or short detache is generally the easiest to play just above the middle of the bow. Since the detache is generally played in the middle or upper half, the hair of the bow should be quite flat on the string.

Many times a smooth detache cannot be done because the fingers are too tight and sometimes even too loose, just the opposite. It has been suggested that if the sound is too loose, the fingers should be tightened with some pressure and added weight to the fingers. Remember the stroke is not simply down and up, but a pull, push feeling in the hand and wrist. If the detache has a tight sound, try loosening the hand somewhat, and playing fast detache notes in the upper half of the bow, with the first finger and thumb only. When you start to feel the required relaxation of the hand, then gradually add the second finger, the third, etc.

For improving the detache sound, it will help if the player thinks very carefully of what is to be done in order to acquire it. Speed, with a lot of bow and without much pressure, nearer the fingerboard, makes the sound become quite light, even delicate; a tone with more pressure and little speed, nearer the bridge, is apt to be more resonant, more concentrated, even brighter in sound. The distance of the bow to the bridge, or the bow to the fingerboard, most assuredly plays a very important role in acquiring a fine detache and a colorful tone.

Chapter 14
LEGATO — SUSTAINED STROKE

The word legato signifies that style in which the tones are sounded in smooth succession. It is often indicated by a slur placed over or under a group of notes, thus to be connected.

There are two important points to be remembered for the mastering of this style of bowing: (1) Passing from one string to another; (2) To change the bow stroke very smoothly, as regards separate bow strokes. A successful rendering of a piece depends upon how smoothly the change of stroke was made.

Legato bowing gives us the beautiful singing tone of the instrument — it is cantabile in its truest sense, you cannot sing on the violin without it. An artist will express himself — speak, plead, make you cry, laugh and play upon your emotions with a beautiful legato stroke.

The legato bowing is one of the strokes most used, and when well played, has a quality of great charm and pleasure. As the means to perfecting the legato, there are basically three very important rules to remember: (1) Do not raise the finger on one string before the tone of the next string sounds; (2) Practice passing from the G to D — A to E — and D to A back to G to D — open strings as well as fingered notes — all played by means of the wrist, supported by the forearm, making very sure that this movement of the arm as it passes over the various strings must be made in an almost imperceptible manner, without any trace of brusqueness. Of considerable help to the student will be to practice the stroke in different tempos, such as half notes, quarter notes, eighths, sixteenths, etc., all with the above mentioned crossing of the strings; (3) Make sure that the forearm is turned inward as the bow reaches the middle, elbow extended out, going on to the point, all on the down bow. In the up bow, return to the frog via the same process. Do not forget, as the forearm turns inward, the hair of the bow starts to flatten out, completely flat at the point. On the up bow, reverse process (as mentioned before).

In learning the art of legato, one must be very careful not to "spend the bow," that is, moving the bow too quickly, especially more frequently on the down bow than on the up bow. This will hurt proper tone production. The bow is to the violinist as the breath is to a wind player. Any good teacher will tell you that to develop bow or breath control for either, practice long notes.

As soon as your eye determines the number of notes bracketed together in the one big slur, your mind should quickly divide the notes evenly in the bow (all according to the number of notes to be played). For example, two half notes, slurred, would indicate half of the bow for each note, etc. Also, if you increase the speed, then obviously, less and less arm would be used with more of the hand stroke coming to the fore, so as to be able to cope with the demands of the speed, freedom and relaxation of the entire arm.

This is the principle we have just learned, "the longer the bow used, the more arm to be used." The quicker the movement of the arm, less bow and arm is used, finally, using a hand motion only.

The short sustained stroke is nothing but a miniature reproduction of the whole bow sustained stroke. The player must decide how much arm or hand or a combination of both, must be used in the shorter stroke. Too much motion and too little pressure will result in a "glassy sound." Do not be afraid to experiment! Practice with either more hand or more arm involved.

A firm belief that is shared by many fine teachers throughout the world is that the art of legato playing is greatly misunderstood by many players. They encounter problems which should never occur if the concept of legato playing is firmly understood.

Let us analyze these points:

Point One: Playing two or more notes in one bow stroke is called legato.

Point Two: This stroke will involve the change of fingers in the left hand, as well as the fingers of the right hand, being involved in the crossing of strings.

Point Three: Now, the trick here is to see to it that the bow should not be disturbed by what the left hand is doing.

General concensus of opinion is to practice legato in these various ways, and if carefully and systematically followed, it will definitely produce good results.

(1) Practice a particular passage with left hand only (no bow). Observe left hand, watch what it is doing. Be sure it is done smoothly.

(2) Now practice same passage with right arm only (no sound), fingers silently going through the passage. Keeping your eye on your bowing arm, watch carefully what it has to do in order to play the passage.

(3) After carefully practicing the above, now put it all together and play the passage.

(4) To actually realize what the right arm is doing and what it takes to produce a legato on one string, consider this attempt. Play long bows

(count four) on a string, then play cluster of 16ths (four to a cluster), same notes, four beats to a measure, on same string. Result? Realizing the bow arm's task is to acheive a smooth legato.

(5) A further aid in developing legato is to play double stops, then playing the double stops as crossing strings, keeping the bow very close to each string. Sometimes, as the crossing is being made, a slight pressure of the forefinger at the moment of crossing will certainly help in maintaining the legato sound. Know your bridge!

(6) Shifting can also be greatly aided by a slight pressure of forefinger at the moment of shifting.

(7) Crossing strings in legato form requires flawless timing between left hand and bow arm. Keeping fingers down as much as possible, not lifting one finger unless the next finger is already down are among the general rules to be observed in order to facilitate a pure legato.

(8) String crossing at the lower part of the bow may prove to be slightly awkward at first, but just keep in mind the use of the finger actions and inward turning of the forearm as the legato crossing is being made. The fourth finger (pinky) of the right hand is the key to the proper balance of the lower part of the bow. Pressured 4th finger.

(9) It will be found that in playing legato strokes near the tip of the bow, a slight pressure on the 1st finger will help to keep the hair upon the strings without any kind of interruption. Decidely flat hair and wood.

(10) Legato stroking near the frog is executed

entirely by the wrist, fingers holding the bow very lightly. Absolutely no arm pressure.

Through the medium of a sustained type of bowing, a cantabile or singing tone is produced. Carefully observing the outstanding features of this stroke, we find:

1. Quality of tone produced.

2. Unbroken contact between bow and string.

3. Evenness of stroke.

4. Balance between bow speed and bow pressure.

The legato form of bowing is the most commonly used, therefore, also the most commonly abused. Remember that the hand extension stroke is highly related to every type of bowing. The hand extension action completes every stroke, but so skillfully coordinated with the main arm that the listener often cannot tell where one begins and the other ends.

Therefore, the sustained separate stroke is an important element in securing continuity of action and is depended upon to join the strokes so as to sustain the character of the tone (not disturbed).

In contrast to the separate detached stroke mentioned above, one note to one stroke, we now arrive at the study of the slurred legato, whereas the term legato implies that the separate tones are bound or joined together, the slur legato indicating how many tones are to be joined and played by one stroke. They may be sounded on the same playing level or the joining together of two or more playing levels.

Unevenness in the legato may be due to unevenness of stroke or carelessness in the joining of the hand extension with the stroke.

The semi-legato is generally played at about the middle of the bow.

The pure legato, between the middle and point of the bow.

To connect slurred tones on the violin is simple when one has solved the problem of crossing strings, but to connect tones between which there is a change of bow stroke is quite difficult and requires great care.

Of considerable help to the player will be the thought that in order to pass from one string to another without a break between the two tones, the arm together with the hand must begin to turn the bow with the rounded motion toward the new string, while still playing the note preceding the change. As a result, when it is time to sound the note on the new string, the bow is already near it. Timing is of the utmost importance and it should be very carefully practiced.

In practicing wrist studies, consider yet another point, that of keeping the bow contact on the inner side of each of the two strings used and not to pass on to the further side. Otherwise, the motion becomes too large and too much vertical action will take place, decidedly a clear waste of movement.

Generally, the smooth change of bow stroke is made by a little movement of the fingers and hand combined. It may vary, however, the finger and hand movement may be longer in rapid and long strokes than in the slow and short stroke. Remember, smooth legato playing, passing from string to string, depends largely on the fingers retaining their place on the strings.

Watch out for this common mistake, which is not too often noticed and corrected, and that is the tendency to shorten or rush the last note or notes before changing strings in a legato form. Evenness must be maintained at all costs.

As the student progresses in the study of the bow arm,

he will gradually acquire the feeling and the realization that to possess a lovely legato, and to make a really favorable impression as a performer, he must avoid monotony and lack of color, making use of the different shadings and various tempos, interpretations, etc.

"To make the violin talk!" Parlando! (To speak) Without the complete control of the bow arm, the student cannot possibly accomplish this.

Theory: Accurate pivoting is a matter of precise timing. The simplest form of pivoting occurs when two adjacent open strings are slurred in the same bow. When single bows are used, the same two notes are by no means so easy. Then the question of timing arises, and the legato is frequently spoiled by late and clumsy pivoting. This also is the worst possible preparation for rapid bowing, when an extensive pivoting movement must often start from the very beginning of a stroke.

To improve your legato, play your scales in slurs of two, three, four, etc., very slowly. The same way for arpeggios. Listen to yourself. Make it sound like a performance! Try it without vibrato, then with vibrato. Play it softly, relax, then loudly, still relaxed.

Look for the area on your strings where your violin sounds best when the bow is placed upon it. The general belief is that most violins will sound so much better if the bow arm does not press, squeeze, etc., on the instrument. Always listen, listen and listen!

Young students are so intensely involved in looking at the notes (their eyes are bulging) that if not called to their attention by the teacher, the art of listening becomes a lost art and as the student gets older, this kind of playing gradually develops into faulty intonation and poor legato playing.

The surface sounds made by the bow as it is drawn

firmly across a string (and even with the greatest it is noticeable) are common to all competent violinists, especially when they are performing in a large concert hall. A great deal of this is probably due to early training, because there are a great number of teachers who insist that the student must always strive for a beautiful tone, exclusive of any and all harshness. Yes, there should be times of big, bold tones, but also times where the composer has indicated small, soft tones, that obviously have to be played with a very delicate touch, a smooth silky sound, with no scratching or harshness of tone.

How hard a violinist can afford to "dig" into his string will naturally depend on his instrument and how much pressure this small instrument can stand before it starts to complain by groaning, with strange scratching sounds, etc.

For heavens sake, the moment you hear such strange scratching noises from your instrument, relax immediately, loosen up, go for the purest sound to be drawn from your instrument.

When playing slurs, avoid crossing strings, such as going directly from the third string as this can cause a faulty slur. Keep slur crossings as near to each other as possible, keeping fingers down, whenever possible.

Most noises occur when the bow has become much too close to the bridge, or when the arm is too heavy at the frog.

Chapter 15
MARTELE — SUSTAINED MARTELE
COLLE — PIQUE

Martele would be defined as "notes struck with special force or hammered." One of the most fundamental of all strokes, sometimes called the "Grandaddy" of bowings, its mastery will benefit the right hand technique to unlimited demands, the detache, staccato, colle, etc.

We will now discuss the martele and present the different theories to the perfection of the stroke, which is also called marcato.

Theory: Martele is nothing but a series of short up and down strokes played at the point or upper half of the bow; they are incisive attack strokes, usually used in forte passages. It is the basis of two other forms of the stroke, the staccato and the "dotted note" strokes which, like the martele, are played at the point or upper third of the bow. Its use presents the additional physical advantage of reinforcing the muscles of the wrist. This stroke is of the utmost importance! Most artists concur on the theory that for the development of an authoritative bow arm, the whole bow martele stroke is considered the most valuable one to learn to do well.

Many students are often taught that the accent of the martele is made by an increased pressure on the bow at the beginning of the note, but quality of sound is to be questioned. Pressure must be applied during the pause between the notes and relaxed at the instant the bow moves. The pressure is applied by the inward turning of the arm, for here is where the source of power for the martele accent is situated. This also helps to eliminate the tiredness usually associated with this type of bowing.

Theory: There are three important points to be remembered: (1) The middle finger of the hand, not the index finger, is the more important of the two fingers. If the student concentrates all the weight in the first finger, the result could be a squeezing of the bow and a tension in the tone; (2) The most important factor in developing a big strong tone is complete relaxation of the right arm and hand; (3) Inward turning of the forearm with the arm and bow at the same level with the nut, not above or below it.

Practicing the martele stroke is highly recommended at the lower half of the bow, this form of martele being termed by many composers as marcato. When performing the martele in very soft passages, be sure that both speed and pressure of bow are decreased. In playing the martele, make sure that each note is played with a separate stroke, short, sharply attacked or accented, with a pause between the notes. Accent the up stroke to counteract a tendency to play the down stroke more strongly, the attack coming from the hand, not from arm or shoulder.

Theory: One fine artist highly recommends the following points, "Using the first two fingers of the right hand to control the entire stroke. Certainly one cannot believe that so much physical strength is required in its performance that it is not possible to get it from the first two fingers. Why not strengthen the first two fingers? Also advises the use of flat hair at the tip, also flattening the wrist. Then, to practice all strokes at the point of the bow, firmly pressing down on each down and up bow, with a definite pause between each stroke and making use of the wrist exclusively to produce the tone desired. Add a slight pressure of the forearm, if wrist alone is not sufficient."

Theory: This stroke should be practiced slowly, due to the stopping and setting of the bow pressure before each stroke. Young students often describe this bowing as "the one where you take more time to get ready than you do to actually play it." The attack of the martele from a stiff or locked position prevents the needed freedom of motion. As one can now see, in a detache stroke the feeling of movement should be between the thumb and second finger. In playing the martele stroke, the required bite should be exerted by the thumb and first finger, while the feeling of movement remains between the thumb and second fingers. The pressure applied is done by the thumb pressing up against the first finger.

Theory: One of the foremost teachers of his time had suggested some very fine practice exercises for the development of tone production, and herewith, we pass them on to you:

(1) Put point of bow on the string, apply much finger pressure, give an up stroke with the whole bow as rapidly as possible, then take thumb off the bow near the end of the stroke. (The bow should then be resting against the little finger side of the palm.)

(2) Use full bow on the down stroke, finishing the tone by wrist extension and thumb release, then return bow upward over strings at once.

(3) Practice down or up strokes, finished by the lifting of the bow off the strings by finger action. First and fourth fingers give a sudden pressure of the bow against the thumb, for the finger lift.

(4) Practice martele stroke, with pressure, stroke and relaxation, with wrist motion of the bow, moving the hand but keeping the arm stiff. This hand martele should be practiced both at the point and frog.

(5) Practice martele with full arm stroke and hand extension, keeping thumb on bow and holding the bow on the strings. This is a very important preparation for legato playing.

(6) Constant hand position may be shown to the pupil by a very slow full stroke. The fingers should have the same position in relation to the bow, at all points of the stroke.

(7) The martele should be practiced with long rests between notes. (Start with short strokes, then gradually playing longer and longer strokes, until the full bow has been reached.)

(8) When crossing strings, the bow should, upon completing the stroke, rest immediately on the string that is to be played next.

To sum up at this point, we must keep in mind a few careful observations.

A. When most of the pressure is not released at the end of the stroke, quality will suffer.

B. Be careful not to apply new pressure before the stroke is finished.

C. No scratchy sounds — made by too much pressure at the instant of stopping.

D .On up bow ending at the frog, lift bow slightly, then reset for down bow, thereby eliminating unusual sounds at the heaviest part of the bow.

E. The shorter the stroke, the more the hand and fingers will become active. Naturally, the long strokes will involve the entire arm.

F. Relaxation of the arm after each stroke is the key to the martele stroke.

Another type of the martele family (though not as often used) is the sustained martele. Briefly, it is a half breed, half detache and half martele. Once the attack is started, the martele is taken over by the detache. There is much more control over this stroke.

Next to last, but not least of the martele family, is the colle. The stroke is done from the air — attack, lift, attack, lift, etc. Generally played in the lower half of the bow, the bowing can be lengthened. At the frog, the fingers and hand are used, more arm with the longer strokes. Recommended practice is to play at the frog, lifting bow after each stroke, back on the string to prepare for the next martele attack. It is a most important bowing, suggested by many teachers for acquiring control of the bow.

The last of the martele family is the pique, a French term meaning sharp, picked, pricked, etc. Each note sounds like the attack in martele, sharp and pointed. Recommended to be played by wrist alone, placing bow on string, attack, then lift bow from string, place bow on string again, attack, lift, etc. This type of bowing can be used preparatory to the flying staccato. Highly recommended is the silent full bow martele — playing the stroke a half inch above the strings, up and down, with no sound. (This stroke should please your next door neighbors!) Seriously, it does produce fine results.

Chapter 16
THE DECISIVE STROKES
GRAND MARTELE — GRAND DETACHE

The theory that detached decisive strokes are the best means of quickly developing right arm control is becoming widely accepted. We are referring to the grand martele and grand detache. Actually, they show only slight differences in general characteristics. Both are decisive forceful strokes, carried out with entire length of bow, freedom of arm movement, and manner of concluding the stroke, either on or off the string. Paying strict attention to the playing level of the stroke and a uniform grip of bow throughout the stroke are also features to be carefully kept in mind.

Personally, I believe the removal of the bow from the string to be the distinguishing feature between the two strokes. In the grand martele, the bow is removed, while in the grand detache, the stroke is concluded on the string.

As a result, the grand martele may therefore be considered the most pronounced example of detached action.

Be very careful in practicing the grand detache, that in stopping short on the string to conclude the stroke, sufficient relaxation and relieving of muscular strain is observed, so as to conclude the stroke with smoothness. If the rigidity of the hand position is still so pronounced that some students cannot carry out the feature of the stroke, then we suggest the following as one way to enforce relaxation of the right arm: "At the conclusion of the down stroke, leave thumb alone, lift the fingers from the bow one at a time in quick succession, permitting them at once to fall back into position without effort. With the release of the first finger, its usual control over the bow is removed.

Then simply replace first finger, etc., on string and start the stroke again. This procedure should certainly help attain the necessary relaxation needed to perform the grand detache.

Tone production may be begun with the martele stroke, given with the full length of the bow.

The French words pousse (pushed) and tire (pulled), and definitely not up bow and down bow, are the proper conception of bowing. Holding the tip of the bow with the left hand, the frog held between thumb and second finger, now endeavor to pull and push against the resistance of the left hand. This will give you the "feel" of the wrist, hand and finger motion needed for most bowings, especially the grand martele and detache.

Theory: Many teachers comment on the close relationship of both strokes and that they are produced in almost the same manner (in the detache, there is no pause). As said, technically, the grand detache is not quite so important as the grand martele, but for tone production studies, it is hard to beat.

Chapter 17
SPICCATO

The definition of spiccato is, "Played entirely with a loose wrist in the middle of the bow, slightly lower part of the bow when tempo is slower. Bow bouncing on and off the string. An Italian word meaning separate or distinct. On any bowed instrument, it would refer to a springing sound in which the bow leaves the string at each stroke."

Again, we will be presenting the various schools of thought on playing spiccato bowings, and in some instances, if it sounds repetitious, it is only because they seem to agree on that one certain point of reference.

Remember that the distinctive description of the two types of fast spiccato and sautille are at times quite arbitrary, which is why we will deal with them separately. Sautille is first cousin to spiccato.

The third general type of bowing is the resilient category (the other two are the decisive and sustained stroke), in which the bow is required to bounce, rebound, etc. This involves a delicately balanced muscular bow control. The resilient bowings are now divided into two general types, (a) played off the strings, by the hand, as in spiccato; or (b) a combination of arm and hand, as in the ricochet, a so called thrown stroke, which we will discuss a little later.

We will now discuss the most distinctive of the resilient bowings, the "spiccato." This is what we consider a major stroke of the bowing family, used very often by the string family, especially the violins. This type of bowing is a "must" for the "fiddler." It is written far too often by the composers to be neglected and not performed well by the individual player.

Theory: One outstanding teacher generally plays it in the middle of the bow (fast tempo), short, without any effort, making use of the wrist only. The effect should be a bouncing, springing bow by means of a very slight detache in the middle. Using a flat hair, wood over the hair, relax pressure of the fingers on the bow and avoid any violent movements of the hand. In the student's earnest endeavor to make the bow bounce as much as possible by main strength, it will have an altogether contrary effect. The stick will make irregular leaps and bounds and the student will find himself unable to master or control it.

So, to review, this style of bowing is executed entirely by the wrist, middle of bow, bow held very loosely between the fingers so that it may jump over the strings without the slightest problem. Bow kept nearer the bridge, elbow drawn close to body. (The above summary is just another spiccato theory.)

Theory: An artist friend of ours has recommended that students practice the spiccato in this order:

A. Practice on open string, middle of bow (detache), the bow well on the string, wrist only. Up and down.

B. After the wrist has gained a certain amount of agility, exercise on two strings may be tried. A to E, G to D strings, etc. (still on the string). Up and down.

C. To obtain the spiccato, all that is now necessary is to relax the pressure of the fingers on the bow. This time, off the strings, both strings, etc. He said, "The faster the stroke, the more you play in the middle of your bow — the slower the spiccato, more of the lower part of the bow is to be used. There is no better exercise for building wrist flexibility than a constant crossing between the same pair of strings. Since the springing stroke is generally made at the middle of the bow, or there about, depending, of course, on just where your bow rebounds most freely, this stroke should not be attempted by anyone who has not first mastered the hand stroke, which, as was pointed out, is made entirely from the wrist."

Theory: From another teacher, "Spiccato should not be tried until the student has become completely at ease with both the decisive and sustained strokes. The procedure involved in string crossing movements must be thoroughly understood before spiccato is attempted, for with uncertainty in the movements, the results are awkward, tensing of arm muscles and worst of all, muscular conflicts, 'in toto,' lack of bow control!"

Another approach to the stroke is to fling bow down on string, allowing it to rebound, with no motion from hand and arm. After bow hits string, it reacts against 1st finger, forcing hand to turn as if pivoting around axis.

The motion is similar to the turning of a door knob. Begin with mechanical bounce, and stay with it until hand and arm relax and permit the bow to carry on. When this step has become easy, add the down and up motion and then the gentle bounce.

There are some sources that teach spiccato as being best with a loose wrist. However, there are others who say a firm wrist if the notes move at a slow speed. As the speed is increased, more wrist and less arm action is used until the bow is doing sautille entirely with the wrist.

The fast spiccato is often called the sautille, while the slow spiccato on the other hand, is founded on the short martele stroke (except that the bow is lifted after each stroke). Besides spiccato, it will sometimes be called sautille, saltado, saltando or pique.

Theory: As one teacher so aptly put it, (1) in spiccato, the bow hair is flat — detache, side of bow; (2) spiccato, wrist is flat — detache, a dropped wrist; (3) spiccato, elbow is lower — detache, elbow is higher.

Theory: The present day form of producing the spiccato requires the use of the forearm more than formerly, when this type of bowing was once looked upon as a wrist movement only. The theory is that at most tempos, the arm is almost always used, and at a very fast tempo, the wrist only is used. Loud tones would require more arm and more hair, soft tones, naturally, more wrist and less arm.

A biting sound of spiccato can be produced with the bow being held vertically above the hair, a soft bounce will occur when the bow stick is tilted towards the fingerboard. Most bows will bounce best at about the middle (it may vary slightly). The present day theory is that as the tempo increases, less bow is used, with the little finger off the stick. In slow tempos, the little finger remains on the stick.

Crossing strings back and forth would require the raising or dropping of the entire arm with only the slight aid of the wrist. Care must be taken to keep the same amount of bow hair in contact with the string or the bounce will become uneven. Keep the bow close to the strings when crossing — the higher the bounce the more likelihood of losing control over the bow. As before, this action is produced by the whole arm, forearm turned inwardly, slight wrist.

To create a more percussive spiccato sound, like an accent, simply raise the bow slightly higher at the frog. When the spiccato is broad and slow, it is played more toward the lower part of the bow — when it is quick or short, it will be generally played at or above the middle.

The greater the speed, the more the shift from arm to hand and fingers. Keep in mind that the tone quality will be greatly influenced by the height of the drop — the higher the bow, the louder and sharper the sound.

It was suggested that the arm be held outward from the body — arm and wrist being held slightly higher. Also, using more bow and less bounce, for better tone quality.

Many of the schools/theories are to practice spiccato in the lower part of the bow, broadly, with arm leading, hand, fingers following, then proceeding onward to the middle with shorter strokes, this time with less arm and more hand and fingers.

Complete control and playing of the spiccato hinges on remembering several rules. (1) At all times, a bouncing bow must have a firm surface against which it will bounce (flat hair and bow). (2) Slow spiccato should be done with a firm right arm. (3) Near the frog, wrist enters into the stroke. (4) At the middle, very little arm movement (fast tempo). (5) At the frog, wrist only is used.

(A) Good dependable hand stroke, short or long, on its proper playing level and on the strings (detache).

(B) Evenly balance distribution of hand and arm, finger and thumb in proper relaxation, so that very little effort is required to suspend bow over the string levels.

(C) Constantly maintain contact with the bounce and string, requiring strict control of muscular action. This timing must be extremely accurate if the string is to be instantaneously responsive.

(D) The grip of the bow must be instantly relaxed the moment the bow touches the string, checking the bounce and permitting the bow to

cling to the string for the desired length of the
stroke. This requires the utmost of mental alert-
ness and attention.

Spiccato, much like the detache and martele, is played
with a separate stroke of the bow, but of course, the tone
quality will be much lighter and brighter, due to the fact
that the bow is constantly brushed against the string. The
arm motions are similar.

Softer passages are played in the middle of the bow,
those requiring more tone, in the lower half. Remember,
the faster the stroke, the less arm motion is used. Very
quick tempo, using only the wrist (sautille).

"Relaxation at all times is the keyword, the player
always being conscious of a free swinging arm."

Theory: The eminent teacher, and one of the foremost
players of this day, Joseph Joachim, explained: "In the slow
or controlled spiccato, the feeling in the hand must be one
of a see-saw type of balance between the first and fourth,
or first, third and fourth fingers. This process must be
accomplished with the fingers exclusively and not with the
forearm. This feeling of the fingers is required in order to
have the bow spring back of its own volition. There should
never be a feeling of lifting the bow from the string."

When playing in the middle of the bow, the down and up
movement of the bow is done with the forearm and the
hand as one unit, with no active motion of the wrist."

Theory: As we approach the frog, the wrist becomes
increasingly active, so that when we are at the frog, the
spiccato is performed entirely with wrist and fingers, and
no forearm. The reason is that in the middle, we must use
the natural bounce of the bow. At the frog, though, an
artificial bounce has to be created. So, in the fast spiccato
or sautille, there is a light pressure between thumb and
first two fingers, complete relaxation of the third and

fourth fingers. Notice the resemblance of fast detache with the spiccato and sautille. Listen carefully to the tone quality, and for a more resonant sound, use more flat hair and do not let it jump too high.

Never attempt spiccato at the point. This again is another type of bowing. Spiccato involves a natural rebounding of the bow, well controlled. This is virtually next to impossible at the point.

To make the bow "dance," it is only necessary to leave the forearm and elbow free, after throwing the bow at the strings from a suitable height by means of pronation. An ineffective slow spiccato usually results from insufficient forearm rotation, the movement is almost entirely across and not sufficiently toward and away from the string. You can always control the degree of elasticity by varying the angle or flatness of the hairs of the bow. The maximum rebound is secured by placing the hairs absolutely flat. If the bow is too lively, it can be curbed by simply tilting the hairs so that fewer of them are in use.

Chapter 18
RICOCHET — SALTATO

The ricochet bowing sounds are similar to sautille, but are thrown or allowed to fall on the string and rebound, many equal notes in one bow. Played mostly down bow.

For this type of bowing, the bow again must be held as lightly as possible, the fingers hardly touching the stick. It will bounce more readily if more hair touches the string than usual. Turning of the bow should be done not by the wrist, but by shifting the hold on the bow.

To start the stroke, raise the bow about a half inch above the strings, let it fall with an elastic movement of the wrist and you will find that it will rebound as far as you freely allow it to do so. At the beginning, it may give you a number of unequal hurried tones, but after a patient period of practice along the lines laid down, you should be able to play two, three, four, etc., in an absolutely rhythmic manner with one bow stroke or any short or long bow that is desired. Remember, very lightly held bow with just enough hold, as to cause the bow to rebound of its own "free will."

The most important thing is to watch that the fingers of the right arm completely relax their grip on the bow after the bow has struck the string. Use only the rotated balanced forearm when throwing the bow on the string.

"Flatten hair, wood directly above it and forearm turned inward, elbow outward."

When performing the three and four string arpeggios, the main bow jumping is done by the upper arm, mistakenly ascribed to the wrist because of the loose throw of the hand, especially at the beginning of the down bow.

By now, we know that to bounce two or more notes with one stroke of the bow (ricochet, etc.), the forearm action will now have to be combined with the hand. All of this is to be done by tapping the bow on the string. All of these actions would have to be under complete control, resulting in a clear, biting attack. This bowing is based entirely on the natural bounce of the stick. Sometimes it has even been called the "uncontrolled" bowing. However, the ricochet can be pretty well controlled by varying the place on the bow and by controlling the height of the bounce, the bounce being faster near the point and slower about the middle. Also, faster when the bounce is not too high, slower with big bounce.

Up to now, if the reader still has problems with the ricochet, it may be due to several factors: bow being held too tightly, entire arm too tense, wrong part of the bow being used for the speed desired, or the bounce being much too high for control.

Again, summing it all up, the saltato or ricochet is technically easy to perform, just remember these points: (1) Hold bow with a very loose wrist. (2) Hold right elbow slightly higher than usual. (3) Rotate forearm inwardly. (4) Drop bow loosely (upper third of bow) onto the string while moving out from that raised elbow with a down bow. (5) Practice on open strings, the "dribbling" or drumming down bow sound.

The really fast springing type of bowing should be done near the point of the bow.

Chapter 19
SAUTILLE

Sautille — a skipping motion, fast spiccato, bow does not really leave the string, sort of half on and half off. Tone quality similar to spiccato, but with a faster tempo, slightly different manner of execution. Another type of jumping bow, accomplished by the resiliency of the stick.

Theory: Played in middle of bow with loose wrist, turning bow so that more hair touches the string, thereby achieving a firm controlled "bounce." Turning of bow towards the bridge is done not by the change of wrist, but by slight shift of grip on the bow. Recommended — to acquire this bowing, start with a short detache in the middle, gradually increasing the speed, holding bow more lightly until it bounces. If in attempting to play the actual sautille or springing bow, the student encounters some difficulty, try lowering the bow slightly toward the next higher string, which would change the angle of your wrist, and should give you good results.

Theory: Sautille can be done by a very rapid rubbing of the middle of bow on the string, with the bow and hair flat. In many cases, the rubbing will be very hard, disregard the unpleasant noises. When you feel that the bow is trying to leave the string, immediately lighten pressure of hand, wrist, and fingers. The entire process is done by very short, short open string practice.

Theory: To practice sautille, use small fast detache movements near the middle of the bow stick, the hair flat. Hold bow lightly, concentrate action on the fingers, which will be doing both a vertical and horizontal motion, more inward turning of the forearm, the balancing point of the hand resting on the index finger.

The third and fourth fingers either off or slightly touching the stick. The failure of sautille to bounce properly may be due to a too firm or heavy grip of the third and fourth fingers. Good suggestion, practice by holding bow between first finger and thumb, gradually adding the second and third fingers, fourth finger being optional. If bow jumps too much, add a little more pressure from index finger.

Avoid violent movements of the hand and the bow will bounce by itself. Try to keep bow in the same place, between bridge and fingerboard, in order to avoid whistling and foreign sounds.

Remember these rules:

1. A fairly tight flat bow and hair.
2. A loosely held flat wrist.
3. A very quick short stroke at about the middle of the bow.

Theory: The following method was suggested to make the bow spring on the string; first, placing bow firmly on the open D string, using the hand stroke, up and down, after several minutes keep shortening the hand stroke until it is less than two inches, start holding bow lightly, quickly take off all pressure of third and fourth fingers from the bow, raising arm a little higher. This should bring about the desired effect, that of the springing stroke. Kreutzer's Etude No. 5 is a good example of practicing this stroke — first with four strokes to each note, then three, then two, and then just one. As we have learned, the bouncing stroke must be well controlled, in the center of the bow. Be careful not to stiffen the wrist, as in all forms of the bow leaving the string, a flexible wrist is very important.

So, to sum up thus far, we have presented four different

"schools or theories" to the reader (some resembling each other), and we have learned that there are two distinct ways of causing the bow to leave the string after each note. The first, used in fast playing, is to set the bow springing through rapid, very short and light up and down strokes. The second, used in less rapid passages, is just bouncing the bow by the hand alone, on some occasions, by the hand and arm combined.

When playing very near the middle and at a rather fast speed, with the bow never fully leaving the string, we have sautille! At slower speeds, the spiccato is used.

A reminder — in the case of sautille bowing, the little finger can be removed with impunity by all players.

Using the forearm rotation will be of considerable help in acquiring the elasticity needed for the sautille.

Remember, the grip of the bow must be very loose and relaxed, concentrating on the thumb and second finger. If you use a tight grip, plus the upper arm swing, the combination is more apt to become a spiccato.

RELAX AT ALL TIMES!

Chapter 20
STACCATO

The solid staccato is a succession of short, crisp, separated notes on one bow, played while the hair of the bow
remains in contact with the string. Staccato is a style of
bowing consisting of two kinds, "firm, solid, and/or flying."
The flying bouncy staccato is where the bow leaves the
string after each note.

In order to keep the following material simple, unclut-
tered and uncomplicated in the readers mind, this chapter
has been divided into two parts. The first part, dealing
primarily with the firm/solid staccato and the second part
with the flying "bouncy" staccato, sometimes known as
"staccato volant."

Before undertaking the study of the staccato, be sure
that you have virtually mastered the marcato/martele
stroke. For within this lies the cliche, "One cannot acquire
a good staccato without a good marcato," or, "it is so
much easier to acquire a good staccato if one has a
good marcato."

Since this section of the chapter will deal primarily with
the firm staccato, let us just dwell briefly on the rest of this
"family." The firm bowings are generally listed as marcato,
martele, martellato, short staccato, grand detache, etc.
Explanation:

    1. Short staccato: Notes are short, forte and
detached.

    2. Slurred staccato: Notes are equally distrib-
uted, rapid, in nice style.

    3. Martellato: Notes are longer time value,

greater volume of tone.

4. Grand detache: Notes are still longer, requiring greater volume of tone.

5. Solid staccato: Played detached, with upper part of bow.

Generally agreed upon are (a) the firm short staccato is best obtained near the point of the bow; (b) the semi-staccato played at about the middle of the bow; (c) bouncing staccato played at the lower half of the bow; (d) that in the class of staccato bowings, all strokes require a clear cut beginning and a pause at the end of each stroke.

No other variety of bowing has been the subject of so many lengthy discussions or such controversial differences of opinion among teachers and players as the solid "staccato." Everyone has an opinion as to the best and easiest way to perform the stroke. One thing we do know for sure is that when played with dash, fervor, excitement and brilliancy, no other stroke in the violin field can compare to the staccato, for the immediate reaction is to sit up and take notice. Very impressive, indeed!

Before proceeding, bear in mind that the following "methods/schools" on performing the staccato will, in the final analysis, be left strictly up to the individual student to decide which of the methods he/she prefers. All of the great violinists seemed to have disagreed as to how best to perform the staccato. A good suggestion would be to try them all, then decide!

Actually, a good staccato is founded on the mastery of the marcato stroke, for staccato bowing is nothing more or less than a succession of slow or rapid marcato strokes played without change of bow direction.

The serious student may encounter some difficulties in staccato, which is readily understandable, especially when their marcato is not fully developed, the difficulties being the motion itself and coordination with the left hand. As many have advocated, practicing on open strings in different rhythmic patterns will help a great deal, in sections of two eighth notes, then three, four, five, etc. (open strings first) then the simple scales can be applied in like fashion. The tense staccato is not to be practiced for too long a period, a few minutes on a regular daily practice schedule is more highly recommended.

From this point on, our controversy starts, how to produce it, how to start it, whether through action of the wrist alone, through wrist and lower arm, fingers only, stiffened upper and lower arm, through means of a stiffened wrist and quivering tremulus action of the upper arm or just with the index finger digging in? And so on, and so on.

First, let us discuss the "stiff arm" method of staccato. A fine example of this type of bowing was that master of the violin, Wieniawski. He was decidely the most brilliant exponent of the staccato stroke, using the upper arm only, stiffening the wrist to a point of actual inflexibility. This method also seemed to have been adopted by Alexander Bloch, Leopold Auer and most of his student artists. Wieniawski's staccato was of astounding rapidity and brilliance. Basically, the stroke should be executed from the shoulder, with a stiff arm. The forearm must be turned inward. A good way of practicing this stroke is to play on open strings, an eighth note played down bow at the upper third of bow, followed by the stiff up bow movement, in clusters of 4, then 8, and finally 16. Use very little bow, the notes sounding crisp and clear. If a tiny space between each note is utilized, use a short, quick abrupt stroke.

Another great performer of this type of staccato once said: "It is a stiff arm stroke and the wrist becomes part of the arm. Just put the bow down on the string, stiffen the arm and go at full speed. Control will come later."

Again, we were told by a very famous teacher that a very
fast or nervous staccato was produced by forgetting about
the scoops, attacks or marcato notes. "Just simply tense
the entire arm from the shoulder to fingertips, which will
help to induce a feeling of trembling, and by maintaining a
constant pressure on the string, the trembling feeling is
passed on to the bow."

Many of the fine performers seem to agree that the fast
staccato can never be accomplished by practicing it slowly!
(It remains your choice.)

Notice this difference. DeBeriot used a stiff wrist and
upper arm; Kreutzer, Spohr and Joachim advocated use of
the wrist alone; while Vieuxtemps used the wrist and forearm! All in their own way produced a brilliant staccato.

To continue, when playing the very fast staccato (nervous), this becomes a general tightening of the upper arm,
no wrist or finger action, slight upward or inward motion
of the elbow, thereby throwing the weight of the arm
toward the first finger of the right hand. Thus, the trembling of the upper part of the arm will be transferred to the
very relaxed hand or wrist. It has been said that this stroke
should be practiced only very quickly and nothing is gained
from practicing it slowly and then gradually getting faster.

A fine violinist friend of ours told us that he practiced a
very fast tremolo at the tip of the bow with the wrist and
flat hair, maintaining the speed of the tremolo, moving the
bow slightly forward with the arm. The up stroke with the
arm cuts off the down stroke of the tremolo. He claimed
this to be the best way to develop a staccato. (Try it.)

For those who are not advanced enough to perform the
staccato bowing, the following procedures may help in
mastering the technical problems involved. This would be
the wrist and finger action as advocated by the opposing
faction — the stiff arm school of players.

To this end it should be taken up and practiced, just as was necessary for the martele. At the start, the separation of the notes should take place very slowly and only after being produced clearly and evenly may the tempo be increased. The staccato is produced by pushing the bow (up) with wrist, forearm and fingers, exerting a short accent-like pressure on the bow for each note, bringing about a distinct and exact separation of each of the notes. This is to be practiced from the point of the bow to the middle of the bow, slowly at first, then gradually increasing speed, always remembering the "accent" for each separated note.

It will seem that this exercise is nothing but a succession of martele up bows strung together on one bow. In the staccato, however, the pressure is not entirely released as it is in the martele, a certain amount must remain on the string even when the bow is still.

It may also help to not only think of it in terms of an accent for each note, but perhaps a scooping motion of the hand (slowly), as if you were scooping up sand on the beach with a little shovel. Eventually, it all becomes a series of short scoopings in one bow. As a suggestion, a metronome should be used to insure absolutely perfect rhythmic control. Remember, for slow practicing, a conscious downward pressing movement of the right first finger can help.

Another artist advocates complete concentration on the first two fingers down (right hand), and the other two fingers off the bow, with a precise pressure for each note — other player's stressing the use of the concentrated use of the index (first) finger mainly.

One very important point to be realized from all these "methods" is the complete understanding of "pressure." Whether it is from the fingers, wrist, forearm, etc., infinite care must be taken, for as in the martele, the pressure must be made while the bow is still, and relaxed the instant it moves.

Perhaps one more approach to the staccato would be the suggestion of placing the center of the bow firmly on the string and gripping the string very strongly. When very sure of the grip, draw bow briskly to the point, stop, and quickly pause just long enough to immediately grip the string for the up stroke. Try 8 to 16 sixteenth notes to a stroke.

The short strokes are much more difficult to perform, because of the greater rapidity of tempo, and may I remind the reader, that the utmost of patience and complete understanding with willingness to experiment is required before one can completely master this stroke. The time put into it will be well worth the effort. It may take a week, a month or a year, but with patience and thoughtful care the staccato can be acquired by everyone.

Touching briefly on a rarely used type of bowing (strictly a terrific piece of show off bow technique to impress fellow colleagues), the down bow staccato, in which additional difficulties are encountered which require careful attention.

The strokes at the start are to be made from the middle to the point of the bow, and may in time (after sufficient practice) gradually start at the frog. To obtain the firmness, the strokes should be made with the wrist and forearm, for if the wrist alone is used, the bow is more apt to tremble.

For more rapid down bow passages, a very stiffened arm should be used, only, of course, if the player has gained enough experience and confidence from the first mentioned wrist and forearm bowing.

Many fine players have been quite successful producing this type of staccato by merely tilting the wood of the bow towards the bridge (somewhat like cellists).

Heifetz, probably one of the greatest violinists of our time and a player whom fellow artists often would refer to as "Mr. Perfection," had a most unique approach to the playing of the "down bow staccato." His "method" apparently involved pulling downward on the wrist, knuckles held almost at a right angle to the forearm with a rigid right arm executing the movement, thereby obtaining an absolutely sensational brilliant effect. Also recommended is to practice the stroke holding the bow with only the index finger and the thumb, the bow tipped towards your face.

The flying staccato and the flying spiccato have markings similar to the solid staccato. The flying staccato resembles somewhat the solid type except that there is less pressure and the bow leaves the string after each note. The lifting will be very slight and should move very steadily, most of the time performed on the up bow. This stroke is a combination of the two methods, playing from the upper arm as well as from the wrist. It is seldom used in orchestra playing, mostly found in solos, concertos, and sometimes in chamber music.

In the firm staccato, the bow does not leave the string, but grabs it, so to speak. In the flying staccato, the bow is raised in an elastic manner after each note. Without the capability of doing the firm staccato, the player will be hard put in trying to perform the flying staccato.

Visual demonstration of the stroke will be of great service to the student, but in addition, he must have a certain natural feeling for the stroke and a very well trained wrist. The flying staccato can be brought about by the lifting of the bow, after each note, by the hand and fingers instead of the arm, though in certain passages the arm will have to be used, bow pressed rather tightly between the fingers.

In the saltato or arco saltando (bouncing bow), the bow is allowed to draw on the string and rebound of itself, the rebound being aided slightly by the fingers.

The flying spiccato is nothing but a succession of spiccato notes in one bow. The bow, of course, is lifted higher than in the staccato form. When used in a series of small motions with the fingers, it becomes quite effective. If the strokes are larger, the hand and arm must be utilized. This is a most unusual stroke, being that it can seemingly "stay" in one place on the bow and yet perform a long series of notes in one stroke. All of these various fancy strokes can only be accomplished by a great deal of patience, understanding and perserverance on the part of the student. The famous teacher, Joachim, once said, "The study of the bow is a dedication of a lifetime."

Chapter 21
STRING CROSSING

There are three ways by which to transfer playing from one level to another and they are (1) by hand alone, when the crossing is but temporary, (2) by hand and arm, for a more or less extended period, (3) by arm alone, when tempo is very rapid, so that the detail of the hand crossing has to be abandoned, also when playing springing bow arpeggio.

It is very important that the student become most familiar with these forms of string crossing, especially when to apply them. When they apply the above, they will have learned the art of elimination of all undesired muscular resistance, and the prevention of conflict due to the illogical movements of arm and hand.

Explanation of (1): Actually, a correct position of the hand in its relationship to bow, arm and string makes it possible to reach and control three strings without calling the arm into action. These transitory positions of the hand, above and below the normal playing of the middle string, are not sufficiently recognized and employed by most violinists. Only by means of the transitory positions can the violinist eliminate a feeling of awkwardness from constantly bringing the entire arm into action for every change of playing level. Again, the ability to transfer the bow from the highest to the lowest string level (G to E) or when skipping one intervening level (D to E or G to A), depends upon your ability to relax the arm and complete the string crossing with the hand.

Discussing (2) (by arm and hand), two elements of

direction are entailed in these crossing movements. They are stroke and string level. The crossing may take place:

    A. On the down bow, or on the up bow.

    B. From a higher to a lower level, or from a lower to a higher level.

The highest level, considering the position of the hand, is that for the G string, the lowest string. The lowest level is also the highest string.

Let us take the higher to lower level, on the down bow. Start the down stroke on the higher level, the hand movement completing the stroke, then utter relaxation. While in this relaxed condition, the arm quickly drops without effort to the lower level. After the arm has established itself on the new level, the hand follows and resumes its normal relationship to arm and string.

Only when hand and arm are in position on the new playing level, and the arm is in readiness to continue with the next stroke on the new level, has the crossing movement been completed. When this process has been analyzed in detail, the player will have eliminated one of the most disturbing factors in the right arm, provided he understands that the string crossing is not complete until the normal position is regained.

The passing from the lower to the higher level is the exact opposite, the bow arm always going on to the next string before the hand, and not playing the next note until the hand attains the level of the arm.

Discussing (3), the arm thus may be said to anticipate each change of level. When the hand has returned to its normal relationship to the arm and the playing level, then and only then is the playing on the new level resumed.

During all crossing movements, the grip of the bow remains unchanged.

Master the down bow crossings first, then the up bow

crossings.

All of the above suggestions bring us up to one of the most important parts of string crossing, the arpeggio!

Summing it all up, to perfect the art of string crossing in legato form, the hand is to be held so that three strings are within reach of the bow, without any arm motion; that is, when playing on one string, the hand is held at such a level that it can make the bow reach a higher string by dropping or a lower string by raising the bow, without change of arm level. If the crossing is allowed to call for too much arm motion, awkwardness will result.

As an artist commented to the question of string crossing with the wrist or arm movement, "the answer lies in the time value of the notes being played. Generally, more wrist on the quicker notes, more arm movement on the slower notes, thereby insuring the breadth of the tone."

When a neighboring string is fouled in rapid passage work, the cause is generally an unsuitable height of the elbow, the upper arm is misplaced in relation to the string, which is being played at the time. Keep elbow at same level with the second knuckle of the hand.

Theory: On large string crossings (when more than one string is crossed), the right elbow should be leading the arm. Do not move your violin, only the right arm should be moving. You must understand and feel that the arm has a different level for each string. So, large string crossings are done with entire arm as one piece. The actual crossing itself is done very quickly.

Small string crossings (undulating strokes) are done with hand only, no arm motion. Passing from one string to another, legato or separately, the movement of the bow must not be seen, the hair almost resting upon two strings at the same time.

Since string crossings involve either more wrist and no

arm or less wrist and more arm, the most important point to remember is, as you are practicing this stroke (large or small crossings), observe your right arm, do not drop further than the level of the strings involved, or, by the same token, do not raise arm higher than the strings involved. Too wide a swing is deadly.

Theory: The basis of string crossing, especially in legato form, requires the apparent understanding of the inward turning of the forearm, elbow outward. The best way to acquire the necessary smoothness in string crossing is to practice scales and, especially a lot of arpeggios, in a moderate tempo, keeping your eye on your right arm for proper level of string and smoothness of tone. When crossing is written softly, use more wrist, for the arm motion produces more tone.

Again, just a few rules to remember in the crossing: (A) In a quick tempo at the upper half, use a vertical movement of the wrist; when near the frog, use the roll of the lower arm in the elbow joint; (B) In a slow tempo between the middle and point, roll the upper arm in the shoulder joint; from the middle to the frog, use the roll of the lower arm in the elbow joint.

Do not make the slow change of string with the wrist, because in this case the wrist comes to lie either higher or lower than the fingers, whereas for fine bow production, we badly need the straightness of the hand and lower arm. In the overall picture, it is the tempo indicated which is the determining factor for the correct playing of change of string.

The correct crossing should always be in a wavy fashion (as little arm movement as possible), almost like drawing your bow in a straight line, never in an angular manner.

The playing of slurred passages which cross several strings is more likely to suffer from excessive wrist and finger action than from the reverse. For this reason, it is wise to develop such passages in the early stages with little bow length, however, long, slowly played bows in slow (adagio) tempo can be tried with much advantage; a firm bow pressure is maintained, while the hand is constantly tracing a continuous curve.

"When crossing strings, proper and exact amount of space must be observed between each string. To wit; if at the heel of the bow, four inches is used in crossing strings, the hand must travel four inches, likewise the same amount of four inches for the elbow."

No bowing method will be consistently successful which fails to recognize that movements can only become equally facile on all strings by allowing the upper arm absolute freedom.

When crossing strings slowly, especially in arpeggio work, play close to the bridge, each note becoming much clearer. When crossing strings rapidly, move bow closer to fingerboard, thereby obtaining very good results.

Chapter 22
ARPEGGIO — SAUTILLE — SPRINGING

Arpeggio — played entirely with a loose wrist, inward turning of arm in the middle, just adding to it the crossing of three or four strings, sometimes on, sometimes off.

Theory: This stroke is produced in accordance with the principles by which the ricochet-saltato is played. Two important points to remember are, first, that in order to facilitate your arpeggio work, you should first start to study it legato, to accustom yourself to passing over the four strings with equalized pressure on the down and up bow. Second, the bow stick should be slightly tilted toward the bridge when starting on the G string and very full hair or flat bow when playing on the E string. This will help to equalize the arpeggio, giving the highest note or string the quality needed, otherwise the tone on the high register is inevitably weak and thin.

Play the legato arpeggio without any forcing of the hand, using the upper half of the bow. The bow arm should be raised accordingly with a slight attack on the G string as you start the stroke, lowering the arm slightly as you reach the A and E strings. After you have attained complete confidence in the legato form of the arpeggio, now you may try the bouncing arpeggio. Attacking the lower note first (like an accent) with an elastic wrist stroke in the down bow, so that it will come off as it should, the up bow should become the rebound.

Theory: Some students may still have difficulty controlling the bounce; it is then recommended that they play the down bow stroke (4 strings) by itself, then stop; play the up bow stroke by itself, then stop; again, the down stroke, stop, up stroke, stop, etc., working along this line until the surety and confidence has been acquired, finally putting both strokes together, with no stops in between, making sure the hair is flat, wood directly over hair, arm turned inward.

Theory: When plenty of tone is required, it is then recommended that you play the arpeggio in the lower half of the bow, not forgetting the inward turning of forearm. There is no doubt that the daily practice of arpeggios are among the finest exercises for the development of your bowing technique. Also, try experimenting by starting some arpeggios up bow instead of down bow, the resulting tone quality may surprise you.

Theory: In a spiccato or sautille arpeggio on three or four strings, the wrist movement is used only on the highest and lowest tone of each arpeggio. This brings about an extension movement, off the string, which in turn enables the wrist to start the return in the opposite direction and accent it. The intervening notes are played with the bow carried along by the arm, the rebound aiding the lift. No wrist movement is needed for this.

Naturally, for fast arpeggios, less length of bow and less arm effort is needed. If the tones after the first are produced wholly by the rebound of the bow, the result is called thrown spiccato or ricochet or sautille. The force of the first note is regulated by the number following it in a single stroke. And so, the wrist gives the first note and the arm the intermediate tones.

Slurred Spring Bow: The throwing of the bow on the strings, the elasticity of the bow doing the springing or bouncing. The thrown arpeggio is mostly used when the tempo is much too slow to use the sautille. They are very similar in technique, except, in the thrown stroke, the little finger is left on the bow, whereas in the sautille and ricochet, the little finger is left off the stick.

The main reason players will have trouble with the springing bow is that they use too much physical effort. In addition, the bouncing should be perfectly balanced and not allowed to stray too far from the middle of the bow. Keep in mind that the main action is of the upper arm. It has often been mistakenly ascribed to the wrist because a loose throw of the hand is often used to assist the jumping.

Keep in mind the following hints regarding arpeggios: (a) generally use a minimum of bow; (b) timing of the lifting motion taking place as regularly as possible without interruption; (c) the use of a combination of different bowings with arpeggios is probably one of the finest sources of material for the right arm; (d) know the shape of your bridge very well — the playing of a well rounded arpeggio's "life" depends on your ability to analyze the cuts in the bridge and the relationship of the strings to each other; (e) during the thrown arpeggio, your little finger rests on the stick, while in the springing arpeggio, the little finger is off the stick; (f) in doing bouncing arpeggios, turn the bow edgewise, toward the bridge; and (g) the slower the notes are written, the higher the bow is raised, the swifter the notes, the closer the bow remains to the string.

Chapter 23
CHORDS

Theory: The acquisition of a fine command of the bow in all chord work depends chiefly upon an elementary study of combining speed and pressure of the bow upon two strings. As an example, the natural tendency of all inexperienced players is to force the bow quickly from the D to the E string. This is the result of being unsure, anxious and unaware of the degrees of pressure required in the playing of three and four string chords.

For example, to cross over from the D to the E string does not require a leap of any kind, one merely discontinues the pressure on the D string and without releasing the A string, forms its new relationship with the E string, the main thought in the player's mind should always be that of drawing the bow, just as he would do if he wished to produce a fine singing tone on one string.

Eliminate the thought of leaping from the D to E string, simply realizing that it is only necessary to slightly lower the arm to reach the E. Combined with the A, you will in time establish the physical agility and feeling in both wrist and arm for purity in the playing of chords. "Pressure, release; pressure, release, etc., combined with absolute smoothness of bow, will show fine results."

Theory: The study of the full or unbroken chord which demands the simultaneous production of either three or four notes of a harmonic structure presents serious problems for both the fingers and bow arm. The word "simultaneous" is misapplied to some extent to chord playing, for it is physically impossible to literally lay on all strings at the same time. To some degree, a four string chord is necessarily broken — the bottom two notes moving to the upper two notes. The rounded form of the bridge means that no human arm, however highly trained, can play on the four strings simultaneously (only on a flat bridge).

However, drawing the bow simultaneously on three strings is an entirely different matter. Many fine examples of this type of three string chord playing are brilliantly shown in the 6 Sonatas of Bach — especially the famous "Chaconne." Here, the player is frequently required to display his bow arm skill plus finger technique, and as the reader realizes, the effects obtained are magnificent when performed by a well trained arm.

To say that all three string chords are to be played simultaneously would be stating it incorrectly, as it would be virtually impossible to lay down any rule by which the player could be governed.

Breaking or not breaking the three string chord would depend on the experience, musicianship and the personal taste of the performer, all of these being deciding factors.

Theory: In ordinary playing, the bow is tilted away from the bridge. For chords, however, the hand is tilted somewhat backward and the wrist is held quite low. This procedure is adapted to those chords whose notes are all equally important.

The whole bow is used from extreme frog to extreme point, with a full movement of the whole arm for whole, half or quarter notes. This kind of bowing is the most used in all compositions for violin. The important point in this is to keep the bow on the string, the tone being continuous and flowing. Violinists as a general rule use too little of the bow.

Theory: As is generally known, the three principal types of chords are the broken chord, the unbroken chord and

the turned chord, each of them being played with a different approach. If the lower notes are played before the beat
and the upper notes on the beat, then it is a broken chord.
If all notes are played together or the lower notes are on
the beat and higher notes coming after, then it is an
unbroken chord. If played with a note besides the top note
being on top at the end of chord, then it can be called a
turned chord (not often used).

The four note broken chord is the one most commonly
used. Principally, downward motion of the whole arm,
inward turning of the forearm as you cross the strings, the
elbow dropping slightly, is the form best suited for this
chord. Try playing these chords from the air, rather than
from a position on the string. Be careful not to play chords
with a high elbow because of the uneven weight distribution of the arm. Keep the elbow slightly lower than the
wrist. Sustained chords are much easier to play if they are
done nearer the fingerboard rather than the bridge. Playing at the frog and close to the bridge is much too heavy a
sound, probably a trifle scratchy. Chords in soft expression
should be played at middle of bow.

Theory: Depending on the shape of your bridge — high
arch bridge, play chords near the fingerboard — a rather
flat bridge, play chord near the bridge; if the bridge is
"normally" rounded, the bow then is placed midway
between fingerboard and bridge.

Getting ready for the chord (if there is time) by resting
the bow on the strings before actually playing the chord,
gives the player the opportunity to observe his hand and
arm. By observation, more control and quality of sound
can be obtained.

General concensus of opinion is that short, detached
three part chords are played unbroken. If the same chord
is long or sustained, then the chord has to be broken

(played as a four part chord — bottom two, top two). All four part chords should be broken (with exceptions).

The playing of short, three part chords is at the lower part or frog, the bow being firmly gripped at the frog, elbow out, then firmly gripping all three strings simultaneously.

String crossing is more easily done if there is a slight falling of the entire arm. The saying is "greater the pressure, the faster the bow should move."

There are some exceptions to the rule of playing chords, particularly in slow, sustained parts. The three part chords (as previously mentioned) will be played as 2 + 2, but the four part chords should many times be played as 3 + 2, especially in places where the upper tone or tones have to be held a little longer (Bach, Brahms). This interpretation will be left up to the understanding of the player toward the composer.

Theory: As we all know, up bow chords are used much less than down bow chords. Starting at the point, the bow should really grip the strings very firmly, with entirely flat hair, as the bow moves, the whole arm should fall quickly to the higher strings. The three and four part chords are played along the style of the down bow chords (together or broken).

Playing chords well, undoubtedly, is of great value to the technique of bowing, for it helps to develop the feel, shading and delicate control needed to produce fine sounding chords in the study of tones.

The student should remember that when one plays short three note chords as a unit or simultaneously, this can more easily be accomplished by exerting sufficient pressure with the bow upon the middle string of the chord!

As always, play with relaxed shoulder!

Just as a reminder, in playing three note chords, for example, make sure that your eye observes the hair of the bow touching the three strings simultaneously. In all chord playing, when practicing, it will be of considerable help to constantly observe the hair contact on the strings.

Two other techniques of chord playing, which require special training, are the consecutive down stroke as well as the up and down stroke. Practice these strokes very slowly at first, and gradually increase in speed. Relaxing the shoulder will solve your difficulty when playing these strokes at the frog. These chords are to be played simul-taneously or broken, depending on the ability and musicianship of the player and his own interpretation of the composer's work.

The question of whether, in a succession of chords, the player should alternately employ the down and up bow or down strokes only, is not always clear even to experienced violinists. Many times the composer will express his feelings by marking in down bows, but not infrequently, the decision is left to the discretion of the player. If one would play the final chords in "Saint-Saens Capriccio" alternately down and up instead of all down bows, we would certainly question his musicianship, even though we certainly would be impressed with his technical skill. In its finality, this resolves itself into a question of musicianship, judgment and your individual interpretation of the composer's work.

In playing up bow chords, the quick dropping of the whole arm itself, without any wrist action, will certainly help the more advanced student, especially when performing any of the Bach Sonatas.

Chapter 24
DYNAMICS

One of the most important results of a fine bow arm is the ability to perform dynamics. Without it, you become an interpreter of music, the conductor screams at you for lack of it, even the composer (if he were alive) would hate you for your lack of playing his dynamics. Most assuredly, your nuance, phrasing and parlando (to speak) would be missing from your playing. Very, very dull, indeed.

What are dynamics? Basically, they are (a) the loudest tone produced by the greatest amount of bow pressure; (b) the softest tone produced by the least amount of bow pressure; (c) as pressure decreases, bow moves closer to fingerboard; (d) as pressure increases, bow moves closer to the bridge; (e) for loud tone, use more bow, more hair of bow; and (f) for soft tone, use very little bow, less hair of bow.

The ability to go from loud to soft or, soft to loud, is what constitutes dynamics. In the simplest of terms, to play forte (loud), the following rules apply: Exert pressure on bow. Keep bow close to the bridge. Use as much bow as possible. To play piano (softly): Keep bow closer to fingerboard. Use as little bow as possible. Exert little pressure on bow.

Violin sound, violin playing, can be very boring if all the above terms are not utilized to their fullest extent. Sing, always sing, but do not forget to shade! A painting done strictly in a single color surely would not be too pleasing to the average eye.

Chapter 25
PRACTICING

Theory: Practicing is an art. It should be learned early in life, while habits are forming. The first step is to learn how to practice with the mind as well as with the fingers and the bow. This means the ability of oneself to first recognize that which immediately requires practice.

As you first pick up a new piece of music, something you have never played before, don't endeavor to play it — look it over, picture the phrases in your mind, observe all the signs and markings, every fingering and bowing. After all these things have been pictured in your mind, then and only then, should the real practice with bow and fingers begin.

Then comes the first rule of all practice: "Play slowly, painfully slow. Not just once through, but many, many times and it may be for days. More pieces are spoiled beyond remedy for pupils through premature attempts at playing them 'up to tempo' than by any other fault." This holds true, unfortunately, in many of our school orchestras, where tempos taken by the school orchestra are far beyond the capability of the students (even after many weeks). Just what does this mania for speed in schools prove? A great deal of poor intonation for one thing, and never a real grasp of the appreciation of the music being played. May I hasten to add, that this fortunately does not apply to all schools.

Playing everything too fast is a bad habit and can in time become a regular part of your daily practice.

Use the slowness of performance as an opportunity for

fast thinking, being watchful, critical and correcting fingers and bow mechanisms, remembering that every piece or passage, every bowing style well mastered, serves as a stepping stone to the next more difficult one.

Theory: Constantly think and listen. A certain dexterity of fingers and bow arm can be acquired by endless and brainless repetition; and may yield some degree of gratification to its possessor, but unless used for higher musical ends, it is valueless. Think and listen while practicing, for in fact, when you have repetition of passages with faulty intonation and an unrelaxed or stiffened arm, it becomes harmful; unless you do think and listen, the practice tends to more securely establish the enemy it is supposed to conquer.

Master bowing difficulties first. The bow is your noblest but strongest foe, until you have turned it into a friend. In most cases the stumbling block for the bow will be found to lie in sluggish string crossings which prevent synchronization between bowing and fingering.

Take a few difficult bars at a time and stick with each one until mastered, then put the whole phrase together, so you can play the whole concept smoothly.

Be satisfied with slow progress. An impatient pupil is a sore trial for the conscientious and experienced teacher, but one who argues is worse!

"Listen, observe, think and remember — say little!" It is a small thing to say "I thank you," but you cannot pay your teacher in any other coin for the interest, love and enthusiasm he throws into his work with you, yet these inspirational qualities are the very ones which may benefit you the most.

Theory: From a world famous teacher comes the suggestion to practice from two to three hours a day, but to break up the hours into half hour segments, some in the

morning, some in the afternoon. This is entirely up to
the individual.

Be enthusiastic about your work. Remember that there
is good practicing and bad practicing, and unfortunately,
the sad truth is that bad is far more common than good.
Some of the problems of the students' practicing can honestly be placed on the shoulders of the teacher for his
failure in pointing out the techniques of good practicing,
working more efficiently at home, and that practicing is a
continuation of the lesson which the teacher had played
and illustrated for him. Possibly the worst thing that a
private teacher can do to a student is to limit himself to
just pointing out his mistakes and not showing him the
proper way of practicing at home. The result is that the
whole week goes by and the student is still not improving.
This can go on for months and months, nay, even years. In
many, many instances, fine talent is being discouraged and
frustrated by the student's inability to improve. "Teach the
student the technique of good practicing at home."

Theory: For the student, here are some sound basic
rules to carefully observe — when, how and what to
practice:

A. Absolute concentration on what you are
doing, for if you feel that you have lost your
concentration, forget it, walk away from it, come
back to it later. Without the necessary concentration, you are just wasting your time and effort.

B. Vary your practicing by starting it differ-
ently each day, start with scales today, tomorrow
do the scales last, etc. Mix it up. That way the
practicing does not become boring, it remains
fresh and more interesting, like a new challenge,
also greatly aiding your ability to concentrate.

C. The matter of, "How many hours should

I practice?" should be left up to the discretion
of the student, what his school schedule is, does
he work after school, what about his social
activities? How much time left to practice? The
rule of thumb is, systematic regular daily period,
absolute concentration, and an intense desire to
play well. Two to three hours should more
than suffice.

Theory: Briefly summing it up, only one question
remains, and that is, what to practice? Generally, one
assumes that the student is studying with a private
teacher. In that case, the teacher will certainly refer you to
the material you need and will in all probability suggest
what you should be practicing. If you are fortunate enough
to have a fine teacher (one who is both a good player and a
good analyst), hang on to him, treasure him, for indeed, he
is a "rare specimen" in our present day culture.

For the student who does not, for some reason or
another, have a private teacher, the following patterns are
generally acceptable: (1) scales and arpeggios in all keys;
(2) all sorts of bow exercises in conjunction with the
scales; (3) etudes such as Wohlfahrt, Kayser, Kreutzer, etc.,
depending on the level of the student; (4) compositions,
pieces with piano, suitable to play at your level. For more
detailed information, look in the back pages under "Practice Material." (Chapter 31)

Chapter 26
BOWING FAULTS

It is almost a minor tragedy to discover that after many years of study, violinists become well aware that all is not right with their bowing. The faults have to be found and corrected.

Many teachers claim that the faults lie in the lack of control of the wrist or the wrist and finger motion, others claim that the problem is in the right elbow, possibly held too low, the elbow being on the same level as the second knuckle.

It is generally accepted that if the player has a good whole bow martele, a flexible and easy going wrist and finger motion with a quick, clean detache in the lower half of the bow, that he has nothing radically wrong with his bowing technique.

Many other faults mentioned here can be corrected, as long as one knows where and what to observe.

Fault: Inability to produce a smooth legato.

Correction: Concentrate on the principal of round bowing.

Fault: Difficulty in effecting a smooth, noiseless change of bow.

Correction: Careful attention to wrist and finger motion at both ends of stick, being aware of the importance of lightening the bow pressure at the frog.

Fault: Poor tone production, scratching, boring sound.

Correction: Too heavy a bow pressure, especially in the lower half of the bow, also undue pressure from the forearm. Make sure wrist and fingers are absolutely relaxed,

forearm turned inward (rotary movement), observe carefully this natural turning in of the forearm, no pressure is
required. As the bow goes downward, if left alone, the arm
will turn inward by itself.

Fault: Weakening of both volume and quality of tone as
the point is reached.

Correction: This is caused by insufficient bow pressure,
the bow stick at the upper half should be tilted towards the
players face, playing with the bow hair very flat on the
string. Helpful hint — practice marcato at upper third of
the bow, with flat hair and tilted stick towards bridge.

Fault: Scratching.

Correction: Do not play too close to the bridge.

Fault: Dull Tone.

Correction: Playing too near the fingerboard. Move back
toward center.

Fault: Hard tone.

Correction: Playing near the bridge, too much pressure.
Loosen up.

Fault: Tonal faults.

Correction: Generally due to a wrong choice of the point
of contact between bow and string. This should be easily
recognized by the player and corrected immediately.

If the player asks himself these questions, he will most
certainly improve his bowing technique:

1. Is the bow pressure too heavy or too light?

2. Is too much or too little bow being used?
   Most times the fault will be too much.

3. Point of contact. Is the bow too near the
   bridge, or on top of fingerboard?

Listen constantly to your playing, does the tone please
you, does the technique flow smoothly? Develop the habit
of constantly being critical of your playing, never being
satisfied with your tone quality, but ultimately knowing

that they are only bowing problems that have to be corrected. With all this in mind, you are now well on the road to recovery and winding up with a fine bowing arm, hopefully acquiring "Mastery of the Bow."

Chapter 27
DAILY DOZEN

Depending, of course, on the degree of concentration and understanding of the player, the following is a list of valuable bowing hints which, if practiced daily, will give the player an enormous improvement in bowing technique.

1. Long sustained tones, especially on G string, very evenly drawn, slowly, anywhere from 10 to 30 seconds.

2. Whole bow martele, with 4 second pause between each stroke. Also going form G to A string and D to E string, using any combination of notes.

3. Martele played in the upper third of bow, again, making use of a definite pause between each stroke — the arm must be turned inward, elbow out, when practicing this stroke — it will help to develop tone in the upper part of the bow.

4. At the frog, play a scale in groups of 4 eighth notes, such as four G's, four A's, four B's, four C's, etc., involving wrist and finger action only, no arm, using side of hair, and no more than 3 or 4 inches of bow at the frog.

5. At the frog, play scales, with the bow lifted after each stroke, about 4 inches above the string. Make sure the bow is placed back on the string after each stroke, so that each stroke is started cleanly.

6. Using all martele strokes, play scales, at the tip, first note separate, next two notes tied, again, next two notes tied, etc. Called the Viotti bowing. For practicing purposes, use Kreutzer Study #2, 3, 5, and 8.

7. Same as above, only this time, tie every two notes (no separate notes), marcato, at the tip.

8. To obtain control and agility in the middle of the bow, practice in groups of four — one down and three up bow spiccato in the middle, wrist only, no arm. On the string, solid sound on the down strokes, then the bounce.

9. Resting bow in the middle for 1 minute, then at the frog for 1 minute, same way at the point. Utilize all strings with thirds, sixths, octaves, etc. No sound.

10. Play all your long slurred passages much slower than actually written — this demands much more control of the right arm. Play near the bridge.

11. Long bows, starting at the frog, very soft, gradually getting louder and louder as you reach the point. At the point, reverse the process, going from loud to very soft at the frog. To be done very slowly.

12. Practice your fast passages with spiccato, keep bow as close to the strings as possible, low fingers, nearer the fingerboard, then repeat the passage closer to the bridge.

13. Full bow marcatos half inch above the strings, making no sound. Slowly.

14. Playing arpeggios half inch above the strings, making no sound, very slowly.

15. Favor most etudes by playing them more at the frog. Very smooth changes at the frog, arm held at the same level as the 2nd knuckle.

Chapter 28
HINTS

Ten Practice Rules for Violinists

1. Concentrate. Concentrate your thoughts on your work. One hour of absorbed practice is worth forty of the casual sort.

2. Play in Tune. The worst of all violinistic crimes is to be untrue to pitch.

3. Practice Scales Religiously. Play them slowly and with perfect evenness, both as to fingering and bowing.

4. Slow Practice. Practice slowly all difficult or intricate passages.

5. Long Bows. Practice long bows slowly, slowly, slowly. Draw out the tone. Pull it out, but never press it out or squeeze the string. By pressing the string, you nullify the natural vibration. DON'T.

6. Memorize. Memorize everything you can or as much as you can, especially difficult passages. This will vastly improve your playing.

7. Think. Keep in mind the structure of the composition while practicing difficult passages, phrases, etc. Keep each measure mentally in its proper place.

8. To Play Before. Try to play your studies or pieces in their entirety before any long suffering friend who will listen. You will be amazed at the sore spots that will reveal themselves, make it your business to heal them as quickly as possible.

9. Listen. Hear other violinists. You will listen in spite of yourself. Then apply that kind of listening to your own work.

10. Love. Love your instrument as yourself. But love your art more than either. Nothing was ever accomplished without faith and enthusiasm.

Don'ts for Violin Students

1. Don't hurry.

2. Don't drag.

3. Don't blur the passage work.

4. Don't scratch.

5. Don't play absentmindedly or carelessly.

6. Don't leave the hair at either the point or nut of the bow unused, thereby curtailing possibilities in phrasing.

7. Don't leave out the accents and other marks of interpretation.

8. Don't forget that rhythm is the first and most vital element in all arts and most obviously so in music.

9. Don't lose your poise.

10. Don't overdo the vibrato.

11. Don't use the same vibrato in an 18th Century composition that you would use in an intense modern piece.

12. Don't alter the composer's meaning, especially classics.

13. Don't become an abject slave to "playing in" your fingers with scales. Sometimes start your practicing with a difficult passage.

14. Don't play to have a good time. Keep your critical self always alert and watchful.

15. Don't practice 10 hours a day. It will kill all joyousness in your playing. Two to three hours should suffice.

16. Don't forget to think out your interpretation away from your instrument. It is often better than actual practice.

Chapter 29
QUOTES

1. "The most important aspects of violin playing are not the physical movements, but the mental control over them."

2. "The key to complete mastery of violin technique is the relationship of the mind to the muscles or the most common usage, mind over matter."

3. "Good playing is a product of an inevitable consequence of intelligent, well planned practice. Therefore, the prime concern of the violinist should be the acquiring of the art of practicing."

4. "The expressive power of the violin and its kind rests in the management of the bow."

5. "Tone, pitch, and rhythm are the basic elements of all music."

6. "Every shade of the violinists' pressure on the bow is reproduced immediately by the strings."

7. "The soul of the bowing is in the perfectly flexible wrist."

8. "Tone makes the violinist!"

9. "A beautiful tone, perfect intonation, and free elastic bowing are the prime requisites of good violin playing."

10. "Master bowing difficulties first. The bow is your noblest but strongest foe — until you have turned it into a friend."

11. "Because of this subtle transference of the violinist's thought to the strings, every player's tone has its own character. This tone is a reflection of the personality of the player."

12. "Does it make sense to practice bow exercises for ten minutes and then spend the next few hours on left hand technique?"

13. "Heifetz owed much of his success to the ravishing beauty of his tone. Would you like to know the secret of the infinite variety of shades at his command? It is by watching the wrist of his and other great artists bowing arm."

14. "Many years ago a very famous teacher said to his pupil, pointing to the bow, 'There is the master, the fingers of the left hand are but your servants.'"

15. "Take two artists, their sound, phrasing, technique, nuance, differs with each of them. Bowing is the distinguishing mark between them. The greater the artist, the greater and more subtle becomes this distinctive difference."

16. "Increase of tone by an increase of bow speed is, generally speaking, preferable to one attained by pressure."

17. "The faster the tempo, the shorter should be the stroke, and the more moderate the pressure. In a fast tempo, the use of a great pressure compels the shortest of strokes."

18. "As a general rule, the student should try to do everything with as little muscular effort as possible."

19. "Bear in mind that the pressure of the fingers on the string must exceed that of the bow. Strong finger pressure enhances the beauty and the carrying quality of the tone, especially in the higher positions."

20. "Bowing is the beginning and end of the art of violin playing. In the early stages of study, spend many weeks in acquiring a proper elementary use of the bow. You will never regret it!"

21. "A faulty left hand can be set right — a radically faulty bow arm, seldom."

22. "In first attempts at bow control, one should keep

the first finger entirely passive. By nature it is the strongest of the fingers and most ready to put its strength into action, and unless restrained, it will act like a bull in a china shop, until it is balanced by control of the other fingers."

23. "It is an absolute must to do daily bow arm gymnastics before you practice pieces. They should be done before the practice of scales and finger exercises."

24. "The student with the arm well trained and well drilled by daily gymnastics finds his labor greatly reduced."

25. "A common tendency with all beginners is to hold the bow too tightly, causing undue tension and wasteful energy."

26. "Good tone and smooth playing is brought out by the right hand, not the left."

27. "Devote the most practice time to the kind of technique in which you are the least efficient."

28. "With the bow, the player produces; on the fingerboard, he prepares."

29. "The use of the mirror is highly recommended for holding and drawing of the bow. Watch closely in the use of the short and long bow."

30. "When crossing from E to G string, be sure that the arm is raised so as to place it in plane of the G string — same thing in reverse, G to E string."

31. "The up bow staccato will always be easier to play on scales coming down, whereas, the down bow staccato is much easier on the going up scale."

32. "Don't get discouraged. If you cannot play an intricate passage as you think it, write it out on paper from memory. It will help you technically and won't hurt your memory."

33. "Don't get in a rut. If you permit it, your soul will be ground in the wheel of routine. Change your routine from

day to day. Don't start daily practice with scales, start with a concerto, etc."

34. "Don't leave technique to the chance of the movement. Inspiration works unhampered only when technique is adequate and reliable. Technique can only be conquered through tremendous routine."

35. "Don't expect your teacher to do your work for you. He can only be a guide and inspiration. But on you, that is within you, depends your success."

36. "Regularity of practice, inseparable from regularity of lessons, is as much a key to success as talent. Without it, talent will not accomplish much."

37. "It must be remembered that no style of bowing is articulate until there is free articulation of the left hand."

38. "I judge a teacher by the bow arm of his pupils."

39. "The elimination of all unnecessary finger action is important. As there are two motions involved in the raising and lowering of a finger, it follows that every time a finger is raised when it might have remained in its place, a double motion has been made needlessly — thus becoming a serious hindrance to rapid playing."

40. "Shifting — release all pressure of the finger immediately after the hand has started toward the new position, do not, however, raise the finger from the string, move the finger along the surface of the string in a rapid and decided manner and stop with suddenness."

41. "To obtain a graduation of bowing color, one must develop a strong, flexible wrist, plus make use of his aesthetic initiative and imagination."

42. "The foundation of all bow technique is solely the smooth and accentuated detached stroke."

43. "Left hand — each finger, in whatever position the hand may be, should act independently, not drawing the other fingers or the hand from their rightful location."

44. "Place the left hand midway between the two positions involved, so that each of the two fingers concerned will stretch in opposite directions. If one note is in the first position and the other in the third, place the hand in the second position."

45. "Gliding — release slightly the finger pressure on the string, immediately after the hand has started toward the new position. Move the finger along the string in an even, smooth and gentle manner until the new stopping place is reached. The exact point of arrival for the new position should be calculated before beginning the shift, and not in the midst of the movement — the latter method would readily lead to inaccuracy in locating the new position."

46. "Think first, train your ear second, then your fingers."

47. "The secret of expressive violin playing lies in mastering the technique of the bow. By using a 'silent' bow, the student can develop the important art of bowing more quickly and with a great deal less wear on the ear. There are times at which the student cannot practice on the violin without disturbing someone in the house. At other times, he ceases to practice on account of the tiresomeness of hearing so many times over and over the particular strain he is trying to master. In such a case, he should use an extra bow without a particle of rosin on it. With this 'silent' bow, he can go through his bowing studies at will, making scarcely a sound and so develop his technique, playing the most tedious bowing exercises, without annoyance to others or himself."

48. "The elbow should rarely be higher than the hand (except at the point)."

49. "Strength without hardness, flexibility without too great softness."

50. "Perfect intonation is, after all, the result only of absolute concentration of the sense of hearing."

51. "The worst crime is to play notes instead of making music. Playing the violin must be like making love, all or nothing."

52. "It will be found that students having poor intonation are almost without exception individuals possessing indifferent powers of concentration."

53. "It is logical to reason that a student must play his studies so slowly that his mind can consider all the factors of his playing and has ample time to dictate the correction of every fault."

54. "Many faults attributed to the fingers are in reality due to an inadequate bowing technique, which prevents the bow from following the rapid fingers as they change from string to string."

55. "Precise knowledge of what to do and how to do it is the basis of all fine teaching."

56. "There never should be a feeling that you move the bow with the thumb and first finger. The first finger is used only to apply pressure. Pure balance of the bow is still between thumb and second finger."

57. "Those with short fingers, left elbow should be under the violin; having long fingers, elbow held much more to the left."

58. "The faster the tempo, the shorter the bow."

59. "For bow arm development, wrist should be perfectly relaxed. To achieve this, hold the right hand straight out, palm facing floor, then drop the wrist. From that point on, the bow position should start."

60. "I would practice the detache in the middle third of the bow without using the wrist. Make sure that the wrist is relaxed while the real action takes place in the lower arm. As the stroke gets faster and faster, less bow is used, with

the wrist finally taking over completely."

61. "Players should learn to assume the proper mental attitude toward technical problems. They may experience certain difficulties and try to overcome them for many years and suddenly find themselves masters of them, by a changed attitude towards the problem."

62. "One should avoid fingerings which require the bow to cross over one or two strings."

63. "Practicing is an art and somewhat of a science. The first step is to learn how to practice with the mind as well as with the fingers and the bow."

64. "The suitability of a fingering is often decided by the type of bowing required by the passage with which it should agree. A change of bowing in many cases implies a corresponding change of fingering."

65. "More pieces are spoiled for pupils through premature attempts at playing them 'up to time' than by any other fault."

66. "First rules of all practice: Play slowly, painfully slow."

67. "Be satisfied with slow progress if it is steady and sure."

68. "For the conscientious experienced teacher, an impatient pupil is a weary road; but one who argues, that is much worse."

69. "Most artists agree on the theory that the center of balance on the bow is between the thumb and second finger."

70. "Muscular technique is not a matter of muscular development alone, but of mental application. Think the passage first, then play it."

71. "A violinist's entire expression, a violinist's individuality, speaks through the bow arm. Through the bow arm he expresses his innermost feelings and emotions."

72. "When playing in the fifth position, learn to play the fourth and sixth positions by letting hand remain in fifth position."

73. "The greatest players are those with the finest right arms, not with the most skillful left hand."

74. "There is something radically wrong in teaching methods that permit talented students to become obsessed with the idea that rapidity and speed are the great essentials. This very desire to play at fast tempos is responsible for slovenliness in execution, for lack of coordination between the two hands."

75. "Complete relaxation is of the greatest importance in the development of endurance when practicing. A 'perpetuo motion' provides excellent material for development of endurance, remembering to concentrate on maintaining a relaxed left hand and a relaxed right hand."

76. "Why is it that some teachers fail to place more stress on the fundamentals, many of them not understanding the basics of sound teaching, which is sure to obtain the progress the student is looking for?"

77. "Be very careful of half steps, many violinists are guilty of playing half steps flat, especially noticeable when playing with other instruments (like the woodwinds)."

78. "Interesting to note how many players tend to shy away from using the fourth finger. Result, the fourth finger has a tendency to be the 'weak sister of the left hand.'"

79. "Generally speaking, in playing the 'Bach Sonatas,' the slow movements are usually played too slowly, and the fast movements, too fast."

80. "I feel there should be no spiccato in Bach. It does not seem to have been used in that period of time. A sautille perhaps, would be more apropos."

81. "Keep fingerings as simple as possible within the realms of good taste."

82. "One has to learn how to relax the muscles while playing."

83. "One of the major causes of nervousness is lack of preparation."

84. "When crossing a string, hold the last finger down for an instant while playing the first note on the next string. This is of considerable importance in helping to obtain a smooth string change."

85. "There is but one way to shift, with the last finger left before moving down or moving up."

86. "To develop an even tone, it is a good idea to practice long notes on the lowest open strings."

87. "Technique is only a means to an important end; and the student should always remember that the end is: Music, always make music!"

88. "Correcting the jerk of the bow at the frog can be done by simply using less fingers and hand, and more arm movement."

89. "For evenness of sound, start the bow at the frog with less hair, as we pass the middle, flatten the bow hair so that practically all of the hair is being used at the point."

90. "What the embouchure is to the horn player, the hand on the bow is to the violinist."

91. "It really does not matter how long you practice; if you practice with your fingers, no amount is enough; if you practice with your head, two hours is more than enough — daily."

92. "Tone production involves primarily even string vibrations, which depend upon the skill with which arm weight is applied when the bow is drawn."

93. "Years ago, violinists played with what we now consider the old fashioned, high wrist, low elbow bowing, but today, it is more common to teach that the upper arm should be held in such a way that there should be a straight

line between the elbow and the hand (elbow even with the second knuckle)."

94. "Referring to the staccato bowing, the very basis of this stroke is the development of the martele bowing. It is wise to develop a martele bowing at different parts of the bow."

95. "One can over practice, do too much; students who practice many hours are rarely concentrating on what they are doing. Practice as much as you feel you can accomplish with concentration."

96. "Oftentimes I find that it is possible to be nervous about a particular passage. I have often feared a certain passage and have learned from experience that there is only one thing for me to do. I completely change the fingering. Now I find I have an entirely new approach to it, and find myself playing it with ease."

97. "Musical timing and technical timing should coincide, with the bow having to be prepared as in staccato or marcato bowings, before the actual playing of the notes."

98. "Never overpress in playing double stops, thereby avoiding stiffness and cramping of the left hand."

99. "Nothing is worse in violin playing than becoming a slave either to tradition or to habit, thereby falling into a rut, the playing becoming stale. Change fingering and/or bowing, it can become fresh again."

100. "The straight bow stroke from frog to tip is the foundation of the entire bowing technique."

101. "It is most imperative to stress shoulder relaxation, from the very beginning."

102. "Good tone production comes from two areas, the motion of the stroking of the bow at right angle to the string and the relaxed springlike action of the arm and bow."

103. "Whenever one problem is mastered, it is abso-

lutely useless to repeat it over and over again. Leave it alone and proceed to the next problem. Don't waste time."

104. "Scales build intonation and establish the correct frame of the hand."

105. "Early youth is the time when technique grows fastest."

106. "Whenever technical problems are encountered, they must be immediately analyzed to determine the nature of the difficulty."

107. "When playing ascending passages up into the higher positions, you will find it much easier to play if you place your thumb under the neck of the instrument (running in the same direction as the neck) as you reach the third position on your way up."

108. "Too much teaching can be worse than too little."

109. "Fingers in direct contact with the bow is the means by which we transmit our most subtle intentions to the strings."

110. "Minimum effort, and consequently, maximum relaxation, must be the goal."

111. "Let your right arm 'float' in the air, thereby giving an excellent mental picture of a perfectly balanced arm."

112. "The hold of a bow is a balance rather than a grip, and that is why the slight muscular exertion required does not interfere too seriously with the conception of a completely relaxed and balanced arm."

113. "Curved movements are unavoidable in bowing."

114. "We should always think of the upper arm as being moved by the body; the forearm by the upper arm; and the hand by the forearm."

115. "Downward pressure in itself tends to prevent free vibration, and thus strangles the tone."

116. "To perform the highest harmonics successfully, it is necessary to bow very near the bridge."

117. "Forearm rotation furnishes the most rapid means whereby the bow can be taken towards and away from the string (pronating)."

118. "Alterations of tone colour are secured by means of three contributory factors; variation in bow speed, in bow pressure, and in the distance of the bow from the bridge."

119. "The hairs of the bow should be used on edge for pianissimo, and almost flat for fortissimo."

120. "Practice the silent 'drum beat' exercise. Bow in the middle, not sounding, bounce in see-saw fashion, between the first and fourth fingers; complete loosening of the grip between the thumb and second finger in order to leave the play axis of the bow free."

121. "Bowing is obviously more important at the outset than left hand work, because a child cannot be expected to judge intonation before he is able to produce a clear sound."

122. "A perfect technique consists in producing all tones with purity of intonation, tonal beauty, with the shadings and the rhythms as required by the composer."

123. "Tone production is essentially a result of bowing, right arm producing pure vibrations, pleasant sound and command of technique."

124. "The pressure at the point is produced by the index finger, the raising of the entire bow at the nut by the little finger."

125. "Index finger, by pronating, produces the tone— the little finger, by supination, preventing the inferior tone."

126. "Good change of bow is inaudible and well-nigh invisible."

127. "Many fine violinists today have recognized that combined movement of wrist, joint and fingers was the

only way capable of producing an absolutely frictionless, inaudible stroke at the frog."

128. "According to most players, the black rosin is a little more powdery and more effective for artificial hair on the bow, whereas the amber rosin tends to be a bit gummier."

Chapter 30
IMPORTANT BOW TERMS

G — German

F — French

I — Italian

Abstrich — Downbow

Accelerando — Hasten tempo

Am Frosch — Bow at the frog

Am Steg — Bow near bridge, producing a glassy tone.

Anreissen — Forceful attack (G)

Apunta d'Arco — With the point of the bow (I)

Archet — Bow (F)

Arco — Bow

Arpeggio — Bouncing bow stroke with each bounce on a different string

Au Chevalet — Bow, near the bridge, producing a glassy tone

Au Talon — Bow at the frog

Aufstrich — Up bow (G)

Balancement — Tremolo (F)

Beband — Tremolo (G)

Bogen — Bow (G)

Breit gestrichen — Broadly bowed (G)

Cantabile — Singing tone (I)

Chanterelle — Note or passage on the E string

Col legno — Strike string, sideways, with the wood of the bow

Coll Arco — With the bow

Colla punta d'Arco — With the point of the bow

Colle — Pinched stroke at frog, often a series of down bow

strokes

Colpo d'Arco — Stroke of the bow

Coup d'archet — Bow stroke

Detache — Detached, separated bow stroke. Smoothly

Detache Porte — Smoothly connected short strokes of the bow, indicated by dash marks

E'largir — To broaden

En pousse, Poussant — With the up stroke

En tire, tirant — With the down stroke

Flautato — Bowing lightly over the fingerboard (Sul tasto)

Forearm — From elbow to wrist

Frog — The bottom or heel of the bow

Gebunden — Legato

Geschlagen — Tap string with bow stick

Gestrichen — Draw bow stick across the string

Grand detache — Strong penetrating loud tone, each note is attached.

H.B. — Half bow

Heel — The frog or the nut of the bow

Herstrich — Down bow

Hinstrich — Up bow

L.H. — Lower half of bow

Lang — Long (G)

Legato — Smooth, round tone, with detached bow strokes, no perceptible change

Legno — Wood to tap string

M — In the middle

Mano — Hand (I)

Marcato — Accented, emphasized, separate bow stroke (Martele) (I)

Markiert — Marked marcato (G)

Marque — Marked, emphasized (F)

Martele — Hammered, detached stroke, upper half of bow (Marcato) (F)

Martellato — Hammered, detached stroke, upper half of

bow (I)

Mettez la sound — Put on mute (F)

Mettre — Put on mute (F)

Mitte — Middle of bow (G)

Nicht—Not (G)

Niederstrich — Down bow (G)

Nut — The bottom or frog of the bow

Ober — Over, upper (G)

Ohne — Without (G)

Ondule — Undulating tremolo (F)

Otez — Take off (F)

Otez les Sourdines — Take off mute (F)

PT — At the point

Parlando — To speak, repeated smooth pulsation, express
   declamation (I)

Peu d'archet — With small amount of bow (F)

Pesante — Heavy

Pestez — Continuance or remain in the position one is in,
   also simile

Pince — Pinched

Pique — Pointed, sharply marked, somewhat like the
   attack in martele

Pizzacato — Plucking of string (I)

Ponticello — Bow near bridge producing glassy tone (I)

Portato — Somewhat detached, without changing bow
   direction

Pousse — Up bow or push

Punta — Point (La point-tip of the bow) (I)

Ricochet — Thrown bow, rebounding, executed nearer
   the point (I)

Ritard — Slow down

Ritardando — Gradually hold back

Saltando — Bow leaves string by reason of elasticity
   rebound

Saltato — Thrown staccato, upper half of bow, down bow thrown

Sans — Without

Sautant — Bow leaves string by reason of elasticity rebound

Saute — Bow leaves string by reason of elasticity rebound

Sautille — Rapid bounce, half on and half off the string, relies on natural rebound

Schwarmer — Tremolo (G)

Segue — When applied to bowing, has same meaning as simile (same)

Sforzato — SF — With a strong accent, suddenly accented

Simile — Same as before, same bowing, etc.

Slur — Curved line connecting 2 or more notes of different pitch

Son file — Long, sustained tone (long bows)

Sonore — Sonorous, with full tone

Sostenuto — Sustained

Spiccato — Springing sound in which bow leaves string at each stroke

Spitze — Point-at the point (an der spitze) (G)

Springbogen — Bouncing bow (G)

Staccato — Detached, separated, short, abrupt

Steg — Bow near bridge, producing glassy tone (G)

Stentato — Holding back each note (I)

Streich — Bow (G)

Strich — Bow stroke (G)

Sul G — All on G string

Sul ponticello — Bow near bridge, producing glassy tone (I)

Sul tasto — Bow lightly over fingerboard (flautando) (I)

Sur II — On A string-Violin; D String-Viola; D String-Cello

Sur la pont — Bow near the bridge

Sur la Touche — Bow lightly over the fingerboard

Tallone — Frog (I)

Talon — Frog of the bow (I)

Tastiera — Fingerboard (I)

Tenuto — Sustained, held

Tie — Curved line connecting 2 or more notes of a similar
    pitch

Tirato — Down Bow

Touche — Fingerboard

Tremolo — Repeated same tone by rapid up and down of
    bow

U.H. — Upper half of bow

Upper arm — From shoulder down to elbow.

V — Up bow

Vers la Moitie — Towards middle half of bow

W.B. — Whole bow

⊓   — Down bow

Chapter 31
PRACTICE MATERIAL

The following are some of the materials available to the student who is trying to make it on his own (almost impossible).
Elementary
  Dancla Charles — Book I
  Gardner Samuel — Book I
  Muller-Rusch — Book I
  Wohlfahrt — Book I
Intermediate
  Mazas — 40 Studies Op. 36
  Muller-Rusch — Book II and III
  Sevcik, O — Op. I, Part I, Book I
  Schradieck — Book I
  Schradieck — Scale Studies
  Wohlfahrt — Op. 74, Book II, 50 Easy Studies
  Wohlfahrt — Op. 45, Book II, 60 Studies
Intermediate to Advanced
  Kayser — Op. 20-36 Studies
  Schradieck — Book II-School of Violin Technics
  Sevcik, O — Op. I, Part II — School of Violin Technic
  Sevcik, O — Op. I, Part III — School of Violin
    Technics
  Sitt — Op. 32, Book III, 20 Etudes-Sitt — Op. 32,
    Book II, 20 Etudes
Advanced
  Dont — Op. 35, 24 Etudes
  Fiorillo — 36 Studies (after Kreutzer)
  Gavinies — 24 Studies (after Kreutzer)

Hrimaly — Scale Studies
Kreutzer — 42 Studies (a must book)
Mazas — 30 Studies, Op. 36, Book I (before Kreutzer)
Rode — 24 Studies (after Kreutzer)
Special Study
Dounis, D.C. — Op. 12, Artists Technique
Flesch, Carl — Urstudien (Basic Studies)

Finale

When one finally arrives at the last page of a book, one realizes that much that might have been said has been omitted, but that hopefully, the material written will be of some aid, knowledge, and encouragement to many talented students and players.

Any improvement resulting in the student's ability to perform more proficiently is well worth the time and effort put into this work.

Prof. Emery Erdlee

Biographical Data

Professor Emery Erdlee, a dedicated teacher, performer, husband and friend to the music profession, passed
away on January 17, 1986, from a massive heart attack.

Since age five, when he began playing the violin, his love
of music flourished around him. He graduated from Jul-
liard School of Music in New York City, where he studied
under some of the world's finest teachers, such as Toscha
Seidel, Samuel Gardner, Lichtenberg and Leopold Auer,
who was Heifetz's teacher. He went on to play the violin
under the direction of some of the world's greatest symphony conductors. He also was a member of the orchestras
at Radio City Music Hall and NBC Studios.

After coming to Florida due to health reasons in the late
1940's, he became Concertmaster for the Miami Beach
Symphony and the Ft. Lauderdale Symphony, as well as
being Concertmaster for the Miami Opera Orchestra.
Aside from his credits in the different orchestras, Professor Erdlee performed in many Broadway shows and also
for such stars as Frank Sinatra, Jack Benny, Steve and
Eydie Gorme, Dinah Shore, Sammy Davis Jr., Jackie Glea-
son, Marlene Dietrich, and many others. Just three days
prior to his heart attack, he had performed with Doc
Severinson and the South Florida Symphony under Dr.
James Brooks.

As a teacher, Professor Erdlee brought out the best
in his students. His patience with them allowed their
talents to grow. His friendship with them allowed their
lives to develop. Because of his sincere devotion to his

teaching, many of his students received scholarships to such colleges as Peabody, Boston University and the University of Florida.

Because his last words to his son Alan were, "I don't want my work to stop here," his son, Alan and his wife, Helene are setting up the "Emery Erdlee Music Appreciation and Scholarship Foundation," which will benefit his students and fund the publishing of this book, "*The Mastery of the Bow*." The proceeds of the book sales will go into the Scholarship Fund so that the professor's students can continue their education.

Music is the universal language and hopefully we will always support our symphony orchestras and musical endeavors as the professor did.

WHAT OTHERS ARE SAYING

The Mastery of the Bow will improve any violinist's bowing techniques, whether student, teacher or performer. Professor Erdlee's methods are not only precise, but produce a tone that exemplifies a real professional. A great source of information is contained in this book, *The Mastery of the Bow*. I should know, he was my principal violinist for ten years.

Dr. James Brooks, Conductor

The Mastery of the Bow will help you achieve the quality sound that you are looking for.

George T. McNally
Philharmonic Symphony of Florida

The Mastery of the Bow should give violin students insights into an instrument which is so difficult to learn, yet so satisfying when it is thoroughly understood.

Dr. Evan Tow, Student

When someone looks back in his own lifetime, he can speak of one teacher who greatly influenced his life. Emery was and continues to be that teacher.

Charles W. Noble
Conductor and Teacher

Emery Erdlee has been a great inspiration . . . and I will never forget the Professor or his wonderful personality. He will live within me forever.

Amy Peterson, Member
Pittsburgh Youth Symphony